The Paris Agreement

the best chance we have
to save the one planet we've got

by Albert K. Bates

an ecovillage *imprint*

ISBN: 0966931785

ISBN13: 978-0966931785 (ecovillage)

Thank you for your purchase of this book.

To Maurice Strong and Hildur Jackson, who led us here, and bid us keep pushing onward.

Hail the goers!

Acknowledgments:

Thanks in the support of my many friends who assisted and encouraged me in getting this book assembled, edited and published in a mere week. I thank especially Gayla Groom and Kathy Hill for the overnight editing and helpful comments. The team in support at home, in the GEN centers, at Transition Paris, on the ground at Le Bourget and at The Place 2B were doubly helpful: Alisa Sidorenko, Brando Crespi, Camila Olarte Zethelius, Carolyn Monastra, Charlene Caprio, Chris Bird, Christopher Kindig, Claire Greensfelder, Corinne Clough-anowr, Daniel Greenberg, Daniel Jubelirer, Daniel Manicolo, Daniel Trigo, Eric Toensmeier, Etienne LeCompte, Ethan Hirsch-Tauber, Feargal Duff, Ferah Withrow, Geun Jeong, Giovanni Ciarlo, Gloria Flora, Greg Ramsey, Guy Renaud, Hayley Joyell Smith, Heiko Vermeulen, Helen Samuels, Henry Owen, Jan Lundberg, Janelle Kapoor, Jason Deptula, Johanna Pfab, John D. Liu, Joshua Konkankoh, Juliet Duff, Kang Sin Ho, Kosha Anja Joubert, Laura Look, Liliana Lewinski, Maria Ros, Marian Zeitlin, Margarita Zethelius, Maria Cooper, Marie Brelet, Marti, Maurice Phillips, Maya Norton, May East, Niels Baloe, Oliver Gardiner, Ousmane Pame, Paula Vigneault, Peter Bane, Rex Weyler, Richard Siren, Rob Hopkins, Rob Wheeler, Robert Hall, Roger Doudna, Ross Jackson, Sanda Everette, Sarah Queblatin, Scott Shigeoka, Soon Nam, Sonita Mbah, Starhawk, Stephanie Meehan, Stuart Scott, Ted Lazo, Thomas Munier, Tim Clarke, Tobias Ellingsen, and Vita deWaal.

Table of Contents

> *"I cannot say with certainty that we are too late
> to turn this juggernaut around, and if I cannot
> be certain, then my responsibility is to act on
> the premise that we can."*

> *"The outer boundary of what we currently
> believe is feasible is still far short of what we
> actually must do. Moreover, between here and
> there, across the unknown, falls the shadow.*

> *"These talks are not just about streamlining a
> text; they are about realizing, at a deeper level,
> the scope of the problem and the required
> scale for any response."*

> *"This is a true challenge. If the story is told as
> one of avarice, private gain, and
> exceptionalism, the human race will go
> extinct."*

> *"Human beings and material objects no longer
> extend a friendly hand to one another; the
> relationship has become confrontational."*

*"Leave the sticks to others. We are carrot
people."*

*"When we are told the hoop is broken, this is
the meaning. It is not difficult to understand."*

*"The television news on any night is like a
nature hike through the Book of Revelations."*

*"If you manage billions of dollars, pounds,
rubles, or euros of your own or other people's
money, it has by now not escaped your
attention that it is all at risk in a most
profound way."*

*"A good tactic is one your people enjoy. They'll
keep doing it without urging and come back to
do more. They're doing their thing, and will
even suggest better ones."*

*"What is missing from last night's draft, in my
view, was strong, coercive language."*

*"Food security and combating climate change
are complementary; regenerative practices
that store carbon in the soil have the potential
to cool the planet while ending world hunger."*

"We need a revolution in means, not only a revolution in ends."

"The question of feasibility is a completely different thing."

"The COP agreed that the era of fossil energy is over. That is no longer in question. It will end by 2050, if not sooner. The question is how, and the Paris Agreement leaves that to fairy dust."

We are a lucky species in that our optimism is more or less hard-wired.

"You want to be a billionaire? Solve a billion-person problem."

Foreword

In 1979, climatologist James Lovelock sent a hand-drawn graph of carbon-dioxide levels to our tiny Greenpeace office in Vancouver, Canada. I pinned it to the wall and began researching this strange, new ecological threat. At that time, only a few people — including petroleum industry chemists and their bosses — knew about global heating from carbon dioxide. That year, the UN held its first climate conference.

Meanwhile, I had published a story in the *Greenpeace Chronicles* newspaper about Plenty, an inspiring group that helped build water and energy systems for some of the world's poorest communities. One of the Plenty crew, Albert Bates, an accomplished public interest lawyer and permaculturist, had also studied the new ecological threat, and in 1990 he published *Climate in Crisis,* describing the threat of runaway heating. Twenty five years later, in 2015, I met Bates on a boat on the River Seine, among indigenous leaders and ecologists attending the 2015 Paris climate conference.

This new book by Bates, *The Paris Agreement,* tells the story of this long, generational saga to recognize and respond to the urgent ecological threat posed by humanity's waste products in Earth's atmosphere.

This book is important because Bates thoroughly understands that the current international agreement still falls woefully short of what will be required, and yet he succeeds in the difficult challenge of facing this reality, while articulating a path to believe in.

Rex Weyler

Cortes Island, Canada
December, 2015.

Preface

From 1980 to 1989, I collected and analyzed more than 3,000 published studies on climate change. Having received formal training in liberal arts, political science, and law, I was poorly prepared but nonetheless taught myself the arcane language of climate science and how to separate the wheat from the chaff in complicated studies and reports.

At the end of that decade, I wrote a book that sifted all this assembled scientific literature and synthesized it into a statement that any reasonably bright 15-year-old could read and understand. That book, *Climate in Crisis: The Greenhouse Effect and What We Can Do,* still stands up pretty well after 25 years. Many of the unknowns that existed then are known today. Many uncertainties with interpretations suspected but not confirmed have been resolved. Still, new knowledge has brought new questions and, in time, we will discover still more answers. Science never sleeps.

One of the more controversial chapters in that 1990 book was called "Runaway." It described a possible scenario in which positive feedbacks cascaded so quickly that Earth's usual recovery mechanisms would not have time to adjust. In an exceptionally bad run of luck, we could lose the friendly atmosphere that sustains higher life forms and instead be shrouded in thick clouds of carbon dioxide and methane, something akin to the atmosphere of Venus. Today there are a growing number of scientists who think that is where we are headed - that Earth will no longer be able to support large mammals such as ourselves, and we could experience our own mass extinction by as early as 2030.

These kinds of doomsday scenarios are not certainties, and may even be improbable, but they are not impossible, given what we are observing in the natural world today and from what we understand of geophysics. We are in an accelerating pace of change, and unless we can radically shift both the pace and direction, it will not end well.

In 1965, an advisory committee warned Lyndon B. Johnson that the greenhouse effect was a matter of "real concern." With estimated recoverable fossil fuel reserves sufficient to triple atmospheric carbon dioxide, the panel wrote, "Man is unwittingly conducting a vast geophysical experiment." Emissions by the year 2000 could be sufficient to cause "measurable and perhaps marked" climate change, the panel concluded.

Since then, every U.S. President has been warned by the best scientists in the world that the problem is serious and getting rapidly worse. Previous to Barack Obama, no U.S. president except Jimmy Carter had done anything to even slow the problem, and Carter demonstrated what Obama already knows - that it is a political liability even to try.

Someone who foresaw this dilemma early and found himself in a position to do something about it was Maurice Strong, the first Director of the United Nations

Environmental Program. He, more than any single individual, was responsible for establishing the Intergovernmental Panel on Climate Change (IPCC) and the UN Framework Convention on Climate Change (UNFCCC) to bring together science and diplomacy. It was Strong's view that better knowledge would lead to wise and timely action by all the nations of the world working in concert.

At this moment we are only one degree Celsius warmer than normal, and that is not dissimilar to the Medieval Maximum, when the rapid deforestation going on in many parts of the world contributed to a significant warming in Africa and Europe (leading the Moors to invade Spain and parts of France). The Medieval Maximum was finally reversed in the 15th to 18th centuries when initially the burst of reforestation from the Black Death and then the depopulation of the Americas so increased the leafy biomass cover of the planet that it tipped us into the Little Ice Age.

That less-than-one-degree swing between favorable and unfavorable climate conditions that changed the course of history tells us an important truth. We inhabit a fragile world whose habitability for life, especially in its higher forms, should not be taken as a given. The Holocene epoch in which human intelligence evolved was maintained as a delicate balance of photosynthesis and reflection of heat to space that was in significant part moderated by the culture and practices of our ancestors. When they cultivated the herds of the Great Plains using controlled prairie fire, or built the terra preta soils of the Amazon to provide food for their civilizations, they helped to maintain that delicate balance within that one-degree range. We can see from what happened after the Colombian Encounter or the Mongol invasion of Eastern Europe that forests are very powerful moderators of global climate, and that humans have the power, with trees and pastures, to turn the thermostat up or down.

However, one degree is not what has been predicted going forward. In 2009, Woods Hole Research Laboratory and the Massachusetts Institute of Technology released a study involving more than 400 supercomputer runs of the best climate data then available. Conclusion: the effects of climate change have doubled the severity estimated just six years earlier, and the probable median of surface warming by 2100 is 5.2°C, compared to a finding of 2.4°C as recently as 2003. Moreover, the study rated the possibility of warming from 3.5 to 7.4°C by the year 2100 (and still accelerating thereafter) at 90 percent.[1]

Another report that year by the Global Humanitarian Forum found that 300,000 deaths per year are already attributable to climate-change-related weather, food shortages, and disease. That figure could be called our baseline, or background count - of the 20th-century-long experience of a temperature change of less than 1°C.

At 5 to 7 degrees, the current trend would take us to something similar to the Eocene epoch, when crocodiles roamed the arctic regions. However, we have moved the carbonization of the oceans and atmosphere far beyond the levels that pre-existed the Eocene, principally with the extraction of 500 million years of fossil hydrocarbons but also by reckless land use, deforestation and desertification.

---

[1] Prinn, R.G., et al., Scenarios with MIT integrated global systems model: significant global warming regardless of different approaches. *Climatic Change* 104:515-537 (2011)

It will take centuries or millennia for the latent effects of those human-induced factors to fully express themselves. It seems probable that what is coming will be far hotter than the Eocene. That is why the Venus Effect has to be taken seriously.

Despite the poorly informed quality of the climate discussion in the United States, science has already reached a consensus. It took thousands of scientists many decades to reach it, something, by the way, that has never occurred before. Exxon, the Koch brothers, Saudi Arabia, and others have almost unlimited money to spend buying political favors and sowing doubt. Through spending billions of dollars each year - many, many times the amounts that are usually spent on political campaigns - these oil and coal interests have produced a generation of politicians with wacko views of science. It is no accident that in the United States, until recently the world's leading carbon polluter, the key Congressional committees charged with addressing climate change have been disbanded, the US Environmental Protection Agency (EPA) is under attack for regulating carbon, and President Obama has been formally informed, by legislative resolution, that any UN climate agreement forwarded to the Senate will be Dead On Arrival.

Against this backdrop we have the Paris Agreement, which changes everything. How did it come into being? What does it mean for the economies of industrial nations? What are its chances of Senate ratification? What will be its effects on the stock market, on jobs, and on future elections?

In heralding the adoption of the agreement, President Barack Obama said:

[T]his agreement sends a powerful signal that the world is firmly committed to a low-carbon future. And that has the potential to unleash investment and innovation in clean energy at a scale we have never seen before. The targets we've set are bold. And by empowering businesses, scientists, engineers, workers, and the private sector - investors - to work together, this agreement represents the best chance we've had to save the one planet that we've got.

So I believe this moment can be a turning point for the world. We've shown that the world has both the will and the ability to take on this challenge. It won't be easy. Progress won't always come quick. We cannot be complacent. While our generation will see some of the benefits of building a clean energy economy - jobs created and money saved - we may not live to see the full realization of our achievement. But that's okay. What matters is that today we can be more confident that this planet is going to be in better shape for the next generation. And that's what I care about. I imagine taking my grandkids, if I'm lucky enough to have some, to the park someday, and holding their hands, and hearing their laughter, and watching a quiet sunset, all the while knowing that our work today prevented an alternate future that could have been grim; that our work, here and now, gave future generations cleaner air, and cleaner water, and a more sustainable planet. And what could be more important than that?

Today, thanks to strong, principled, American leadership, that's the world that we'll leave to our children - a world that is safer and more secure, more prosperous, and more free. And that is our most important mission in our short time here on this Earth.

While I may not have a crystal ball, I have now been following and reporting this issue for 35 years. This book is my diary of the past year, as I watched the quickening pace of negotiations that led, ultimately, to the adoption of the final text in Paris.

I know that I carry my own biases into this reporting, borne of more than three decades watching politicians and diplomats fiddle while Earth burned. I come not from the world of journalism or academic science, but from a world of permaculture, solar power experiments, and ecovillages[2]; a world that is unknown to most people. My expertise lies in appropriate technology, biophysical economics, and ecological restoration. Because of this, I offer a different point of view than what our readers can easily find in other books in this subject. I write with an opinionated style that some may find difficult to accept, even offensive, but I speak with a passion borne of conviction. I hope this helps deepen your understanding of a complex issue. It is one that will affect you very profoundly in coming years.

Albert Bates

Reserva Yum Balam, México
Sunday, December 13, 2015

---

[2] Intentional communities whose goal is to become more socially, economically and ecologically sustainable.

Friday, November 27, 2015
Cancún, México

Now It Begins

I cannot say with certainty that we are too late to turn this juggernaut around, and if I cannot be certain, then my responsibility is to act on the premise that we can.

Went to bed early, at 8 pm, in order to shift time zones and also rise at 3:30 for the short walk from my hotel to the central bus terminal. As I had expected, it was a fitful sleep after the first few hours, waking constantly to check the time, not trusting the alarm on my iPad. Finally I arose, stuffed my roller bag and left the hotel at 4 am, paid the 64 pesos for the airport bus, and arrived at the airport a little past 5 am. Security was light, but they flagged my Biolite[3] stove and I wound up having to summon the supervisor to explain that I was going to Paris, would be making a presentation there, and needed the device, which removed carbon from the atmosphere while it produced electricity. I showed him the official visa recommendation sent to me from the United Nations, and he let me keep the stove in my carry-on.

I did not want to risk checking bags if I could avoid it, as I would have three airport changes and plenty of opportunities for lost luggage.

Waiting for my flight, I was feeling a little clammy and queasy and wondering if the bite on my shoulder sustained earlier in the week while sleeping under my mosquito net

---

[3] www.biolitestove.com

in my thatched palapa deep in the Yum Balam[4], now with radiating burn and swelling, was from a spider or a scorpion. I hoped it wasn't a sign of dengue. I was listening to an audiobook - the first of Kim Stanley Robinson's trilogy on climate change, *Forty Signs of Rain.*

Guy McPherson[5] says the sixth stage of grieving is gallows humor. The best of doomer porn is that. Robinson uses the human narrative, which also works to ease the pain of hard lessons, running a plotline on genetically modified bacteria that help tree roots lignify and sequester more carbon, and another strain that speeds the carbon uptake by phytoplankton in the oceans. I will want to see where he goes with that, because as near as I can tell, all genetic modification is Snake Oil. It has never done a single thing to improve upon natural selection but is instead excellent at producing nasty and unanticipated side effects.

In his novel, Robinson's scientists hope the new organisms will sequester an extra gigaton per year from the atmosphere to the soil or ocean floor. One scientist asks another whether by loosing these genetic modifications on natural environments they risk a runaway effect that will plunge Earth into an Ice Age. The other scientist says it is worth the risk, and besides, "We know how to add heat."

It is hard to understate the importance of Paris in the history of humanity's short run in the geological history of Earth. It probably rivals the moon landing in that respect. Of course, we said the same of Copenhagen, and there is no denying that in both cases, Copenhagen and Paris, we could

---

[4] mexicancaribbean.com/holbox/points-interes/yum-balam/
[5] guymcpherson.com/climate-chaos/climate-change-summary-and-update/

be considerably too late, the damage is already past repair, and we are just at bedside death vigil now.

Perhaps some of my physical and mental malaise stems from that awareness. No doubt it does. Hard not to be fatalistic here. A shaman in the Amazon, studying my face, told me I was too sad. "I am in mourning," I replied. He took it to mean I had lost a friend or relation. I meant I was in mourning for the planet, but did not explain, because the emotions are the same.

Knowing about what Dr. Thomas Goreau[6] calls "geotherapy," ways of speeding Gaia's healing processes through good land stewardship, much in the same ways that various indigenous societies cultivated their ecosystems for millennia, I cannot say with certainty that we are too late to turn this juggernaut around, and if I cannot be certain, then my responsibility is to act on the premise that we can.

Which brings me to Paris.

---

[6] Thomas J. Goreau, formerly Senior Scientific Affairs Officer at the United Nations Centre for Science and Technology for Development, is currently President of the Global Coral Reef Alliance.

Sunday, February 15, 2015
Bonn, Germany

Unburnable Valentines

The outer boundary of what we currently believe is feasible is still far short of what we actually must do. Moreover, between here and there, across the unknown, falls the shadow."

-Al Gore, Nobel Acceptance, December 10, 2007

Whether you like it or don't, the path back to the Holocene after this brief dalliance with the Anthropocene[7] lies through that big steel and glass edifice at One United Nations Plaza. No amount of biochar and holistic management will get us back to the habitable planet we evolved on without also addressing issues like population, biodiversity, poverty, water, eliminating the twin scourges of nuclear weapons and power, Palestine, central bank financial fraud, or even cyberwar. We have to bake, and then eat, the whole enchilada.

The Climate Action Network, based in Germany, reported this past week, "2015 will be a trek. One summit followed by another, ending with a steep climb to Paris."

The first peak crossed on our pilgrimage was the Ad Hoc Working Group on the Durban Platform for Enhanced Action. Part 8 of the 2d session (ADP 2.8) concluded Friday in a swank resort nestled in Lake Geneva's snowcapped mountains.

---

[7] The 'Anthropocene' is a term widely used since its coining by Paul Crutzen and Eugene Stoermer in 2000 to denote the present time interval, in which many geologically significant conditions and processes are profoundly altered by human activities.

13

The second peak was going on simultaneously in New York at the High Level Thematic Debate on "Means of Implementation for a Transformative Post-2015 Development Agenda" presided over by the President of the General Assembly and the Deputy UN Secretary General. In some ways this arcane debate is more important than the piece of paper that goes to COP-21 in Paris, because the final Convention will only address a post-2020 world and the next five years are critical.

Peak 3 will be reached next month with delegates meeting at the World Conference on Disaster Risk Reduction in Sendai, Japan to finalize a new framework for DRR. The shadows cast by Fukushima over that location should lend perspective as delegates arrive at their penthouses with suitcases stuffed full of bottled water and sandwiches.

Two other summits are coming soon to New York: one about Post-2015 Sustainable Development Goals and one for Development Finance Goals. As we scale these, some paths will cross. And always, in the thin air zone, there are risks of summit storms, avalanches, and landslides.

In 1979 the UN hosted the first World Climate Conference. In 1988 the Intergovernmental Panel on Climate Change (IPCC) was set up, and in 1990 it issued its first assessment. In 1992, at the Earth Summit in Rio, countries joined an international treaty, the United Nations Framework Convention on Climate Change (UNFCCC), to cooperatively consider what they could do to limit climate change and cope with whatever impacts were, by then, already inevitable.

By 1995, most countries had realized that emission reduction targets in the Convention were inadequate. They launched negotiations to strengthen ambition and, two years later, adopted the Kyoto Protocol. The KP legally binds developed countries to targets, and even though the United States did not ratify, it is still legally bound by its ratification of the UN Charter. The Protocol's first commitment period started in 2008 and ended in 2012. Needless to say, the big players - US, UK, Australia, Canada - not only missed the assigned reduction target (4.7% in the case of the US), they had increased emissions by huge amounts and were trying to paper over the embarrassment by moving around dates and bringing in nutty numbers. The second commitment period began in 2013 and will end in 2020.

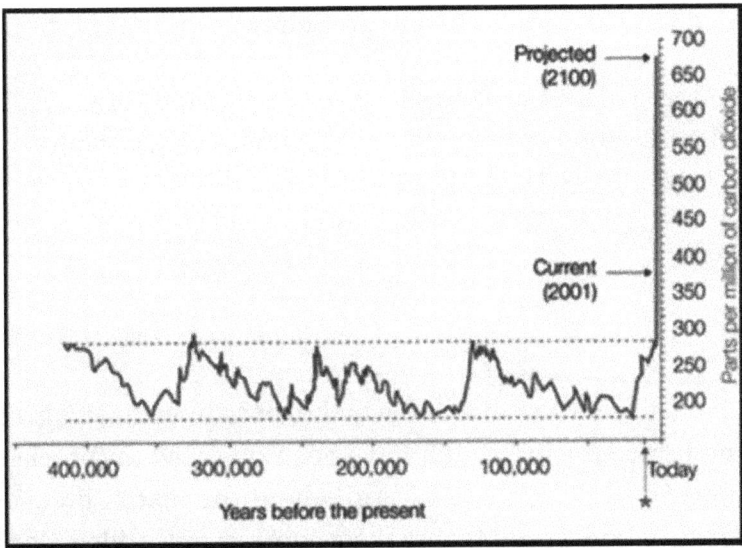

There are now 195 Parties to the Convention and 192 Parties to the KP. The UNFCCC secretariat organizes climate change negotiations called the Conference of the Parties (COP). COP-1 was in Berlin in 1995. COP-21 will be in Paris in December, 2015, and it is planned for that meeting to adopt a legally binding treaty to safely protect the planet from climate change. Right?

> We believe that today, more than ever before, we live in a global and interdependent world. No State can stand wholly alone. We acknowledge that collective security depends on effective cooperation, in accordance with international law, against transnational threats. We recognize that current developments and circumstances require that we urgently build consensus on major threats and challenges. We commit ourselves to translating that consensus into concrete action, including addressing the root causes of those threats and challenges with resolve and determination.

- from the 2005 Heads of State UN Summit Outcome Document

> The second leading delusion in our culture these days, after the wish for a something-for-nothing magic energy rescue remedy, is the idea that we can politically organize our way out of the epochal predicament of civilization that we face.

- James Howard Kunstler

Brackets in the text indicate which words have been agreed to (no brackets) and which have been objected to (brackets). The process of negotiations is all about the text in brackets. Progress is measured by brackets coming off. Added work is measured by brackets going on. In the Ol' Yodler Sausage Shop down in Lake Geneva, one can take giggling children to watch the words come through the grinder and have their appropriate brackets added or subtracted, to better help delegates pick and choose only the best to take home.

WORK OF THE CONTACT GROUP ON ITEM 3
SECTIONS A & B

11 February 2015 @ 08.20h

Option (a): Being guided by the principles of the Convention as set out in its Article 3, including that Parties should protect the climate system for the benefit of present and future generations of humankind, on the basis of equity and in accordance with historical responsibility, common but differentiated responsibilities and the provisions of Article 4 of the Convention / [evolving common but differentiated responsibilities and respective capabilities] / [evolving economic and emission trends] which will continue post-2020, in order to progressively enhance the levels of ambition,

Option (b): In accordance with the principles of the Convention as set out in its Article 3, including in particular that Parties should protect the climate system for the benefit of present and future generations of humankind, on the basis of equity and in accordance with historical responsibility and common but differentiated responsibilities,

[Recognizing the importance of long-range efforts to transition to low-carbon economies, mindful of the global temperature goal of 2°C,]

Option (a): Also recognizing that scenarios consistent with a likely chance of holding the global average temperature increase to below 2°C relative to pre-industrial levels include substantial cuts in anthropogenic greenhouse gas emissions by mid-century and net emission levels near zero gigatons[8] of carbon dioxide equivalent or below in 2100,

Option (b): Also recognizing that scenarios consistent with a likely chance of holding the global average temperature increase to below 2°C or 1.5°C relative to pre-industrial levels include substantial cuts in anthropogenic greenhouse gas emissions by mid-century and zero emissions within the second half of this century,

[Further recognizing that economy-wide emission reduction budgets provide the highest level of clarity, predictability and environmental integrity,]

[Acknowledging that carbon pricing is a key approach for cost-effectiveness of the cuts in global greenhouse gas emissions,]

[Recognizing the special characteristics of land use systems, including the importance of food security, the diversity of global land management systems, and the need to manage multiple sustainability objectives, may require particular consideration within actions under this agreement,]

etc., etc.

Negotiators for 195 countries are trying to craft specific goals, with ways and means ratcheted up or down based upon ongoing, up-to-the-minute authoritative assessments of what works and what doesn't.

Assumptions are to be tested and mandates enforced either by market forces or government regulation, or some

---

[8] gigatonnes: A gigatonne of Carbon dioxide equivalent (GtCO2eq) is a unit used by the UN climate change panel, IPCC, to measure the effect of a technology or process on global warming. 1 billion tonnes.

combination. In the conference chambers, the tensions over language merely reflect subliminal panic as what the numbers actually stand for gnaws at the reptilian brain.

These young mid-level diplomats well know that any gap in mitigation ambition left now makes later adaptation a whole lot more expensive, well nigh impossible. Crafting language like a "public adaptation finance goal" is an attempt to bridge a neurobiological gap between hominid discount-rate calculus and immediate benefit stimulation, particularly in the political arena.

For example, a "loss and damage fund" was not gaining traction amongst the criminal climate syndicate members (you know who you are) because it was punishing rich countries for historical fossil fuel use. The accused demanded waivers, a statute of repose, or blanket amnesty. The same mechanism, once reframed as re-insuring and then relocating vulnerable communities, something that by accounting logic should be given its own source of finance, has few opponents.

One option, backed by strong science, is to replace the $2°C$ limit threshold with $1.5°C$. You could say that once we surpassed 400 parts per million CO_2 in the air, 1.5 became the new 350 on the placards waved outside the building. It was harder to pimp for 350 when everyone was already breathing 400. It is easier to advocate 1.5 because unless you live in Alaska or Greenland, we are still at around 1.0.

The 1.5 trajectory can only be achieved (if at all) through a rapid, nearly instantaneous, phase-out of fossil fuels and phase-in of 100% renewable energy, combined with changes to land use patterns that net-sequester carbon and rebalance the potassium, phosphorus, and nitrogen cycles, mainly by doing away with artificial fertilizers. Still, 1.5, or even 2.0, requires more profound change than the galley-slave delegates, straining at their oars, are revealing, or perhaps even comprehend.

Kate Sheppard, writing for Huffington Post ("Scientists Warn We're Ever-Closer To The Apocalypse") parsed the hidden meaning:

> While world leaders have set a goal of limiting global warming to 2 degrees Celsius (3.6 degrees Fahrenheit), the current emissions trajectory puts the world on path to more like 3 degrees to 8 degrees C (5 degrees to 15 degrees F). "It only took modest 3- to 8-degree warming to bring the world out from the frigid depths of the last ice age," said Sivan Kartha, a senior scientist at the Stockholm Environment Institute specializing in climate risks. Warming on that level again, he said, raises "the specter of a future where the surface of the earth is again radically transformed."

In its most recent report, the Intergovernmental Panel on Climate Change (IPCC) calculated how much carbon we can emit and still keep a decent chance of limiting warming to two degrees above pre-industrial levels. This is known as a carbon budget. Two degrees is the internationally accepted point beyond which climate change risks become unacceptably high, although it was a number set by economists not by climate scientists, and it is based on perceived economic pain thresholds, not ecological survival.

As of 2010, we could release a maximum of about 1000 billion more tons (1000 GtCO2) of carbon dioxide and still have a 50:50 chance of staying below two degrees, according to the IPCC. This is a fallacious statement, as shall be shown later in this book, but it sets in motion a dangerous competition for that limited remaining atmospheric space.

Were we to burn all the world's known oil, gas, and coal reserves, the greenhouse gases released would blow even the fantasy atmospheric budget out of the water. The implication is that any fossil fuels that would take us over-budget will have to be left in the ground. Globally, this equates to 88 percent of the world's known coal reserves, 52 percent of gas, and 35 percent of oil.

Who loses? To start with, the Middle East holds half of total global unburnable oil and gas reserves, with more than 260 billion barrels of oil and nearly 50 trillion cubic meters of gas needing to remain untouched if we're to stay within budget. This "unburnable" fraction equates to two-thirds of the region's gas and 38 percent of oil reserves. Russia accounts for another third of the world's total unburnable gas.

"When I was chief scientific advisor, it was my responsibility to worry about a big outcome with a low probability," Sir David King, the UK's former head scientist, and current envoy for climate change, said this week. "And, what I mean by low probability is 1%. So, when we look at a 1% probability now, we are running the risk of heading towards a 7 degrees Celsius world. And, quite frankly, we ought to worry about that. We can't discount these low risk, high impact events. "

It is unclear whether any life on earth would survive a 7 degrees Celsius temperature rise. And yet, the IPCC's last assessment put our current trajectory, a 2-degree rise by mid-century, 5-degrees by 2100, at an 80% probability.

Climate change is a systemic challenge. Any agreement that does not start with a systemic response simply will not work. That is the juncture we are at, now, as we survey the peaks stretching out ahead on our trek. The fate of our species, and of life on Earth, hangs in the balance, no exaggeration required.

Which brings us a Valentine's Day when it's not just love in the air - but conspiracy. By June we will need commitment. The baby is due in December.

Sunday, June 7, 2015

The Road to Paris

"These talks are not just about streamlining a text; they are about realizing, at a deeper level, the scope of the problem and the required scale for any response."

Newspaper reporting legend Ross Gelbspan[9] once said, lifestyle change is essential, but lifestyle change won't get us out of this climate mess. We need change of the kind that comes only from governments, acting together.

In a larger sense, we need a change of the kind that defies the arc of social history extending back to at least the last Ice Age. Let's face it. Our civilizations are built on organized murder, slavery, and rape of the natural world and of each other. We are a nasty bit of work, we naked apes.

Some of us work towards change at this very cellular level, exploring spiritual and social limitations, working on our group dynamics, getting under our skin with art, music, and spoken word, encouraging the heathen masses to break free from our serpent nature and rise up.

There has always been a tension between "bottom-up" grass roots organizing and "top-down" working for policy changes from the infrastructural brain centers. Most political activists do both, although some will not compromise, on principle, and so fail to even get inside the buildings where decisions are taken. Others, like the Green Party activists in Germany, Ireland and elsewhere, succeed in winning seats

---

[9] en.wikipedia.org/wiki/Ross_Gelbspan

in government only to see their aspirations dashed in the realpolitik of consensus governance.

A study by Professors Martin Gilens and Benjamin Page published last fall in *Perspectives on Politics* [10]challenged the commonly held belief - the story children in Western countries are routinely taught in school - that the way democracies work is by electoral, pluralistic expressions of public opinion.

Gilens and Page studied the progress of 1,779 policy issues through US legislative bodies and compared opinion polls to reach the conclusion that it really doesn't matter what a majority, or even a plurality, of voters want. Thirty percent of bills passed were strongly opposed by the public. Thirty percent of bills passed were strongly favored. Whether the public supports or disdains a particular policy has virtually no effect on its likelihood of becoming law.

> Multivariate analysis indicates that economic elites and organized groups representing business interests have substantial independent impacts on U.S. government policy, while average citizens and mass-based interest groups have little or no independent influence. The results provide substantial support for theories of Economic-Elite Domination and for theories of Biased Pluralism, but not for theories of Majoritarian Electoral Democracy or Majoritarian Pluralism.
>
> - Gilens and Page

---

[10]scholar.princeton.edu/sites/default/files/mgilens/files/gilens_and_page_2014_- testing_theories_of_american_politics.doc.pdf

Welcome to Bonn

Climate change talks rekindled this week in Bonn where representatives from 195 countries are drafting the final negotiating text of the climate change agreement - now at 4,232 lines and 89 pages. Whatever is arrived at will become the next-to-last version for the legally binding treaty that will be signed in Paris this December. Heads of State will be in Paris to pass around flutes of sparkling wine and *hors-d'œuvre* of sausage pâté. Bonn is where the sausage is being stuffed before being hung to cure.

The 21st annual meeting of the parties to the UN Convention on Climate Change (COP21) carries high expectations. Delegates in Bonn are feeling the pressure of disappearing time to finalize the negotiating text and to ensure the new agreement will be legally binding, anchored by honest science, and acceptable to all parties. It is a tall order, but after all, it has been 20 years in the making, so they are not fresh to the process.

The expected draft will likely encourage a massive expansion of renewable energy, greatly improved energy efficiency, a shifting of subsidies from fossil fuels to renewables, a renewed focus on sustainable agricultural practices, and research initiatives to develop zero carbon and net-sequestering infrastructures for all aspects of industrial civilization.

To facilitate that historic switch, overdeveloped country financial support to underdeveloping* countries will be essential. Conventional wisdom would have it that support should come in the forms of technology and capacity building, paid through finance mechanisms only vaguely defined, which is to say, voluntary, self-imposed targets that are neither economically painful nor especially quick.

* We use the phrase "underdeveloping" quite intentionally because it has been our observation that the direction of transformation for much of the world is away from traditional means of providing for the needs of people, which were based on renewable resources and minimal rates of extraction for the non-renewables, towards unsustainable consumerist economies willing to sell their culture, patrimony, rights and finite natural resources for a shot at the Western lifestyle as might be portrayed in reruns of the TV soap, *Dallas.* We also use the term "overdeveloped" to describe industrialized economies that by any measure overspend for the sake of one species and one globalized culture an amount of non-renewable natural resources that is not possible to sustain for more than a short period of time, using the temporary abundance and net energy punch of fossil fuels. We prefer these terms to "developing," "lesser-developed," "developed," "First World," or "Third World," because they indicate more accurately what is really happening. The overdeveloped need to scale back, radically. The underdeveloping need to quit trying to emulate Sweden or Denmark and rediscover their own roots and local economies.

It is key that the Paris treaty include phasing out fossil fuel emissions. To those working in the sausage factory that means phasing in 100% renewable energy, but the Bonn delegates seem a bit deluded in imagining that the old and new are roughly equivalent and we simply have to sweep out those smelly oily rags and uncrate that shiny new solary stuff.

> Making pig iron - the main ingredient in steel - requires blast furnaces. Making cement requires 100-meter-long kilns that operate at 1500 degrees C. In principle it is possible to produce high heat for these purposes with electricity or giant solar collectors, but nobody does it that way now because it would be much more expensive than burning coal or natural gas. Crucially, current manufacturing processes for building solar panels and wind turbines also depend upon high-temperature industrial processes fueled by oil, coal, and natural gas. Again, alternative ways of producing this heat are feasible in principle - but the result would probably be significantly higher-cost solar and wind power. And there are no demonstration projects to show us just how easy or hard this would be.
>
> - Richard Heinberg, Renewable Energy Will Not Support Economic Growth[11]

Killing Nessie

Euen Mearns observed in his May 22, 2015, post, "The Loch Ness Monster of Energy Storage,"[12] that the intermittency of many solar-based renewables places large requirements for storage on a system that has neither the present technology nor any reckoning of the cost. Mearns dissected Scotland's plan to build a gigantic pumped storage hydro scheme, Strath Dearn, in the Monadhliath Mountains, just south of Inverness (population 72,000) on the upper reaches of the River Findhorn.

---

[11] richardheinberg.com
[12] euanmearns.com/the-loch-ness-monster-of-energy-storage/

The scheme proposes to pump seawater from a location on the Moray Firth just east of Inverness to an elevation of about 300 meters (1000 feet) above sea level from where the water will flow south along a canal to the base of a dam at an elevation of about 350 meters where it is pumped into a reservoir with maximum surface elevation of 650 meters. At one level, this is a standard pumped-hydro storage scheme employing the sea as the lower reservoir. The scheme would have two pumping and generating stations, one by the sea and the other at the base of the dam.

The dam would dwarf the Hoover Dam and is of comparable size to Three Gorges in China. Strath Dearn's generating capacity of 132 to 264 GW dwarfs both Hoover and Three Gorges. That is because the reservoir may be emptied and filled regularly, it has a huge head of 650 meters, and flow is not restricted to the flow of a natural river that has been dammed.

Untoward side effects: Loch Ness will become salty from seawater migration. Tectonic stresses caused by loading and unloading the site with 4.4 billion tons of water on a regular basis make living below the dam a risky proposition. Moreover, Mearns calculates that storage on the order of 472 GWh would be required to span low-wind lulls, given present Northern Scottish power demand and zero population growth.

Scaling to a 100% wind-pumped-storage system would increase the planned, already gigantic offshore wind farm from 3 GW to 50 GW. The storage requirement then grows to 50/3 x 472 GWh = 7867 GWh. At that size the proposed reservoir site is not large enough to guarantee uninterrupted supply. So do they power the pumps with coal? Nuclear? Fracked gas?

Which brings up the first of two problems with a UN plan to replace fossil with renewables. Fossil energy is all about converting caloric content of petrified biomass to boil water or otherwise make mechanical or electrical power. Renewables like solar thermal and freshly dried biomass may also work that way, but wind and photovoltaics do not. Fossil energy is the stored sunlight of 500 million years - a great big savings account of light striking some part of our planet for half of each day. Renewables are more like a checking account, we get to use them as they arrive, but savings are pretty much out of the picture.

The second difference is EROEI, or energy return on invested energy. Fossil fuels are very energy dense. A cup of gasoline can take a 2-ton truck over a mountain. How many horses would have to be fed how much grain to accomplish the same task? How many hours of wind generators charging batteries? Sunlight is very distributed and most of it falls on the ocean. Sure, solar input is nearly 4 million exajoules[13] per year, versus only 550 exajoules from all fossil fuel burned to date, but as Charles A.S. Hall, who invented the EROEI concept, says, it is naïve in his opinion "that we can replace fossil fuels with biofuels (most of which have little or no net yield), efficiency, and solar power."

Even more damning, whatever optimistic scenario you might choose, you are likely to soon run into the biggie:

---

[13] The exajoule (EJ) is equal to one quintillion (1018) joules. The 2011 Tohoku earthquake and tsunami in Japan had 1.41 EJ of energy according to its 9.0 on the moment magnitude scale. Energy in the United States used per year is roughly 94 EJ.

the Jevons paradox,[14] in which the efficient use of a resource leads to greater consumption of it - not less. For example, Sweden is a country in which conservation is taken very seriously. A government commission brought together nutritionists and environmental scientists and came up with a nutritious and CO_2-sparing diet. Eva Alfredsson (Green consumption energy use and carbon dioxide emission, 2002) compared Swedes who promised to follow this diet with those who did not. She interviewed both groups frequently and calculated the CO_2 released by each group. She found that the environmentally conscious group did indeed generate less CO_2 and spent less money on food. Looks like win-win, right? But when she looked at total household budgets, she found that the environmentally conscious group spent their saved money in fuel-intensive ways, such as more distant vacations. This effect canceled, and in some cases more than cancelled, their dietary CO_2 savings. About the only environmental benefit was that the first group presumably felt better about their environmental footprint. Genuine energy savings requires a holistic analysis, not Panglossian hope.

- Charles A.S. Hall[15]

Bonn NGOs such as Climate Action Network have called for provisions in the treaty that guarantee sustainable energy for all. By all, do they mean 8 billion people? 12 billion? More? Where do they think that much energy will come from?

Of the countless new initiatives being announced, some are good, and some (let's face it) are greenwashing.

- Climate Action Network[16]

---

[14] Jevons Paradox: synapse-energy.com/sites/default/files/SynapsePaper. 2011-02.33.Jevons-Paradox-and-Energy-Efficiency.11-006.pdf
[15] *Bioscience* 65:6:624 (2015)

Just take food supply, for instance. To bring the climate back in line will require restoring normal carbon and nitrogen flows, and to accomplish that we will need to do what Wendell Berry and Wes Jackson[17] have been recommending - change from a mix of 80% annuals and 20% perennials to the reverse ratio. Tree crops have a lot in common with other forms of renewable energy, because their production is less dense - requiring more land per food calorie produced, although the ecological services produced by forests are incalculable.

> Over 35% of the energy in agriculture is used making nitrogen fertilizers. If this must drop by 90%, as I believe it must, that means creating an agriculture dependent on the cycling of all nutrients, including human waste. It also means having a lot more farmers, at least 10 times as many as at present, perhaps more like 20 times, and all of us will need to live closer to the land that feeds us.
>
> - Wayne Teel[18]

Compensating Loss

For the 2015 agreement to be successful, there needs to be stronger recognition that the effects of climate change will necessitate increased adaptation, away from the memes of "make it happen" industrial civilization and towards the memes of harmony with natural cycles and flows. In Bonn, and equally likely in Paris next December, that discussion is not being had. Instead delegates are trying to anchor the Warsaw mechanism on loss and damage and ensure additional finance. "Loss and damage" places a burden on polluters to compensate those most injured by climate

---

[16] climatenetwork.org
[17] nytimes.com/2009/01/05/opinion/05berry.html
[18] www.jmu.edu/isat/people/faculty/teel-wayne.shtml

change, on the theory that such a policy will put a tangible price on pollution that can begin to value carbon and change the pass-through pollution paradigm for global business and finance.

It is not difficult to foresee problems with the loss and damage approach. So, for instance, who will the US government more likely compensate for loss from climate change, almond farmers in California or drought refugees in Yemen? Apply that same logic for all nations.

These Bonn talks are critical, not just in shaping the Paris agreement, but also in achieving a common understanding on a range of important issues. These talks are not just about streamlining a text; they are about realizing, at a deeper level, the scope of the problem and the required scale for any response.

Sunday, June 14, 2015

Fighting Extinction

"This is a true challenge. If the story is told as one of avarice, private gain, and exceptionalism,[19] the human race will go extinct."

At the G7 last week, the leading industrial nations agreed to cut greenhouse gases by phasing out the use of fossil fuels by the end of the century. While that seem to many, ourselves included, as whistling past the graveyard, the mainstream press and many climate organizations are hailing the diplomatic triumph of German Chancellor Angela Merkel in bringing fossil foot-draggers Australia, Japan, and Canada to a "Jesus, the climate!" moment.

On the final day of G7 talks in their Bavarian castle, and before rushing off to the secretive Bilderberg Group[20] meeting, Merkel said the leaders had committed themselves to the need to "decarbonize the global economy *in the course of this century.*" They also agreed on a global target for limiting the rise in average global temperatures to a maximum of 2°C over pre-industrial levels, oblivious of the contradiction in those two positions.

Two weeks ago, at the Petersberg Climate Dialogue,[21] Chancellor Merkel called upon the overdeveloped countries to draft a roadmap of how to meet the $100

---

[19] Exceptionalism is the perception that a country, society, institution, movement, or time period is "exceptional" (i.e., unusual or extraordinary) in some way and thus does not need to conform to normal rules or general principles.
[20] The Bilderberg Group, Bilderberg conference, Bilderberg meetings, or Bilderberg Club is an annual private conference of 120 to 150 people of the European and North American political elite, experts from industry, finance, academia, and the media, established in 1954.
[21] bmub.bund.de/en/topics/climate-energy/climate/international-climate-policy/ petersberg-climate-dialogue/

billion commitment Hillary Clinton offered underdeveloping countries to acquiesce to President Obama's counter-Kyoto strategy in Copenhagen in 2009.

For five years now, the US has declined to present its thoughts on how to finance such a plan, and not having one has undermined trust in both the UN process and the United States. At home, Obama's popularity ratings are now below those of George W. Bush in his final year. The President's legacy is likely to be that his name becomes synonymous with loss of trust. Merkel's is likely to be associated with loss of ambition.

In fact, let us apply Merkel as the denomination for degrees of warming expected to result from heel-dragging for the next 85 years. Thus, a rise of one degree this coming century would be 1 Merkel. Six degrees would be 6 Merkels, and so on.

Scientific consensus recently concluded that even if CO_2 and other greenhouse gases were stabilized in a time short of 85 years, surface air temperatures and sea levels will continue rising for at least another century and probably several. This means that even if we moved from fossil fuels to 100% renewable energy by 2030 or 2050, further impacts on people and ecosystems will continue unabated. Hurricanes will continue to strengthen. Heat transfer between Atlantic and Pacific across the Arctic may reveal a new tipping point. Both the Jet Stream and the Atlantic Conveyor[22] will break weirdness records.

---

[22] carbonbrief.org/the-atlantic-conveyor-belt-and-climate-10-years-of-the-rapid- project

This might cause one to despair utterly, and then to psychologically block the consequences and perhaps even party like it's 1999. Some speculate that is already what is going on at 1600 Pennsylvania Avenue and 10 Downing Street. This assumes they are already in the acceptance mode of grieving for near-term human extinction. In our view, that assumption is flawed and anybody's despair for our race is premature. Killian O'Brien, from the Permaculture and Resilience Initiative in Detroit, writes:

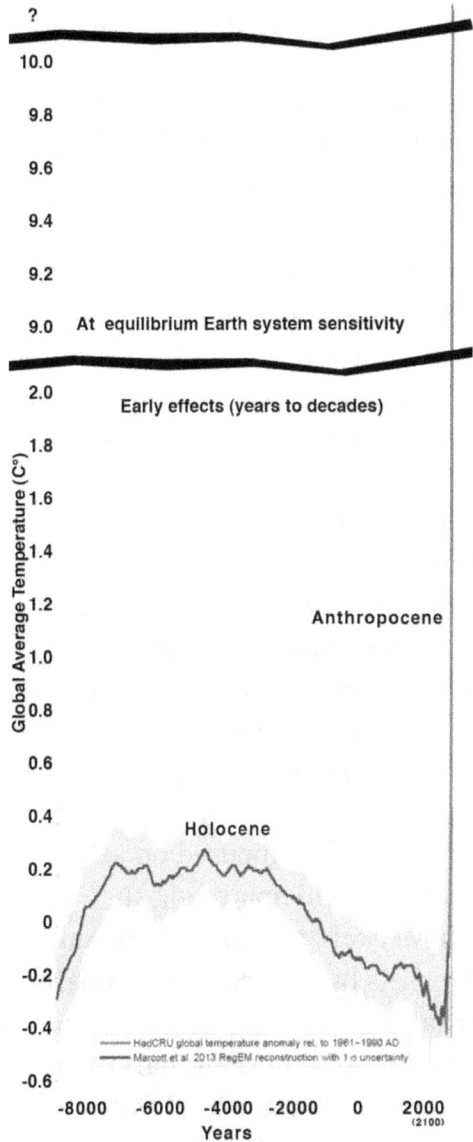

[A] last resort mindset [is] inappropriate when return to a stable Anthropocene, largely de-mechanized and far simpler than OECD nations currently enjoy, is still at least theoretically possible. Given it is feasible to return to sub-300 ppm by 2100, if not far sooner, and even to the mid-to-low 200s, which would bring on cooling, giving up (or "going into hospice," as Guy McPherson puts it), is an unethical, even immoral, suggestion, is it not?

John Holdren, who as White House Science Advisor has the President's ear, should be whispering words to the effect that a global fossil fuel extraction levy, applied at the ridiculously low price of $2/ton of CO_2 equivalent, could easily generate $50 billion a year. That levy would need to increase substantially year on year as we phase out fossil fuels, but it would shift the cost of fossil fuels from the victims to the industry and feedback favorably to accelerate the phase-out.

If the ultimate objective of the UN Convention is to repair the climate, not just to seem to be doing something, it would require actually reversing greenhouse gas (GHG) emissions and taking down concentrations to pre-industrial levels. Step one: zero GHG. Full stop. Step two: go beyond zero, to net-sequestration techniques like biochar, living roofs, bioenergy-to-carbon-storage, and regrarian farming.[23]

The IPCC has focused on setting a goal of 2°C for absolute increase, understanding that we are already at 0.8-1.1°C (call it 1 Merkel), and on our current trajectory we could see 4 Merkels by mid-century globally, and up to 10 Merkels in local regions, such as Mombasa, Mumbai, Damascus, and Beijing. At 2 Merkels, half the world's coral reefs will disappear, small island states and populous coastlines will be submerged, Brazil's soils will go from sink to source, and many indigenous societies will go extinct.

---

[23] permaculture.co.uk/videos/regrarian-vision-restoring-earth-perennial-polycultures

Even to have a 2-Merkel limit begs the question of whether we are aiming to achieve that with a probability of 90%, 66%, or something less, and what might each of those require? A 25-50% probability might require achieving net sequestration in something like 10 years (by 2025). Do non-scientists really appreciate what that means? Even to limit warming below 3°C a radical transformation of capitalism will be necessary.

The Bonn draft text, taking its G7 cue, supports phasing out fossil fuel emissions and transitioning (equitably) to 100% renewable energy by ... 2100? 2050? - That will be the central Paris negotiating point if the G7 and Bilderberg conferences didn't already decide it. Given what we know about the net energy of renewables and Jevons paradox from the Swedish study mentioned in the preceding chapter, it is hard to imagine even a 2050 target representing anything less than 3 Merkels.

Progressive nations like Switzerland plan to reduce emissions by 50% from 1990 levels by 2030, with 30% to be achieved domestically, and the rest through offsets (paying other countries to reduce). This is 10% more ambitious than the EU as a whole, but as the Climate Action Network asks, "If the whole world needs to decarbonize by mid-century, what makes Switzerland think there will be enough offsets available?"

Some, like India and Japan, believe that fossil fuels can be used for some time to come and we will still achieve a 2°C target. India is expanding its coal-fired electric grid by leaps and bounds. Japan is massively subsidizing a coal build-out to help underdeveloping countries further underdevelop and covertly plans to frack SE Asia, on the way derailing antifracking laws, which is a lot of what TPP,[24] TTPP[25] and TiSA[26] are about. Either these countries have a steep learning curve to even comprehend the science, or less charitably, they are merely partying hard towards the Apocalypse.

Japan's PM predicts that by fifteen years from now, 20-22% of his country's electricity will be sourced from nuclear power, despite Fukushima. Coal will provide 26% more energy than renewables in 2030, and extending the operation of old nuclear power plants to 60 years and/or building new nuclear plants is slated to fill any gaps. Good luck with all that. We are getting our protest bandana out of mothballs.

To accord with both ethics and science, OECD[27] countries should cut emissions by 106-128% immediately, the IPCC[28] reports. If that seems extreme, it really is not such a heavy lift, policy-and-popularity-wise. The current $5.3 trillion fossil fuel industry subsidy for 2015 - $10 million per minute - is greater than the total health spending of all the world's governments.

Or compare the cost of Exxon bag money to the cost of the Iraq War, at about $1 trillion per year (and a civilian death toll of an estimated 176,000 to 189,000) - about $1.9 million per minute (although arguably the Iraq War was another fossil fuel subsidy). Subsidizing fossil fuels is like running 5 Iraq wars simultaneously, for the next 85 years!

---

[24] en.wikipedia.org/wiki/Trans-Pacific_Partnership
[25] en.wikipedia.org/wiki/Transatlantic_Trade_and_Investment_Partnership
[26] en.wikipedia.org/wiki/Trade_in_Services_Agreement
[27] oecd.org/
[28] The IPCC assesses the scientific, technical and socio-economic information relevant for the understanding of the risk of human-induced climate change.

But remember the Gilens and Page study, described in the previous chapter. Whether the public supports or disdains a particular policy has no effect on its likelihood of becoming law. The same is true of international law.

> Algeria: "Thank you Mr. President and fellow representatives. I am very glad to talk to you about my country's opinions on unsustainability. It seems as if we are running out of water. And all of our schemes to try to combat energy and renewable resources and climate change - we just need more money. We need more cash. We can use it to come up with new solutions. If only we had more money and investment we could solve all of these problems. If only there was more money we could combat the food issues, the people starving all over the world; hungry, hungry people everywhere."

> - *Extraenvironmentalist* Episode #86, Slow Money Part C (May 26, 2015).

Imagine a group of people in a disaster shelter. If they go outside they will not likely survive, but to stay within means learning to get along, despite their differences. Two of the people are very wealthy, and they inherited that wealth by their parents enslaving or otherwise mistreating the parents of several of the other people in the shelter, engendering feelings that linger as simmering anger.

But, those two people are learned and skilled at the process of organizing groups to work towards a common goal, and they get everyone to agree to join and discuss what needs to be done. Certain things are obvious priorities: food, water, sewage management, personal security, and first aid for the injured. Other things, like working through the emotions of those old hatreds, are less immediate but still need to be addressed for the process to move along.

Many in the group feel that although they have not achieved the wealth of the two wealthiest, they are on the path to achieving it, or were before the disaster struck, and when the disaster is over, they still intend to pursue that goal.

What happens? Every issue that the group takes up - from the smallest to the largest - seems to arouse animosity more than a spirit of cooperation. The two wealthiest, and many of the would-be wealthy, feel sorry for those who have nothing, but they are not willing to share the food and water they have brought with them. They are happy to provide first aid assistance, but reluctant to have hands-on involvement in pollution management, infrastructure maintenance, and health care, other than by designing systems on paper, and they would like to be paid for that.

The poorest, many of whom are used to maintaining good hygiene despite difficult circumstances, are unwilling to perform work for the wealthy that the wealthy are unwilling to perform for themselves. They would prefer to suffer from bad sanitation than from indignity.

In recent issue of *Rolling Stone*, an article looking at geoengineering[29] provided a similar example:

> Gavin Schmidt, a climate modeler at the NASA Goddard Institute for Space Studies, offers a simple analogy to illustrate the point. "Think of the climate as a small boat on a rather choppy ocean," Schmidt wrote recently. "Under normal circumstances the boat will rock to and fro, and there is a finite risk that the boat could be overturned by a

---

[29] Geoengineering is the artificial modification of Earths climate systems through two primary ideologies, Solar Radiation Management (SRM) and Carbon Dioxide Removal (CDR)

rogue wave. But now one of the passengers has decided to stand up and is deliberately rocking the boat ever more violently. Someone suggests that this is likely to increase the chances of the boat capsizing. Another passenger then proposes that with his knowledge of chaotic dynamics he can counterbalance the first passenger and, indeed, counter the natural rocking caused by the waves. But to do so he needs a huge array of sensors and enormous computational resources to be ready to react efficiently but still wouldn't be able to guarantee absolute stability, and indeed, since the system is untested, it might make things worse.

"So," Schmidt concluded, "is the answer to a known and increasing human influence on climate an ever more elaborate system to control the climate? Or should the person rocking the boat just sit down?"

These things play out on the international scale just as they play out in a small group. Unless differences can be put aside, as they were not in Bonn but must be in Paris, there is little hope for the survival of our species, and many others.

If, on the other hand, these things can be put aside for this moment, and we can find common ground and a spirit of shared sacrifice, much is yet possible. This is a true challenge. If the story that is told is one of avarice, private gain, and exceptionalism, the human race will go extinct. For this story to end happily it must be a story of our noblest attributes, elevating us above our history.

In his message to COP20 in Lima, Pope Francis said there is a "clear, definitive and ineluctable ethical imperative to act." In 4 days, on June 18, Francis will issue a new encyclical, *"Laudato Si,"* on the future of our planet and people. It will speak of climate in the context of human moral development. It could not be more on point.

The Gift of Clear Mind: Laudato Si'

"Human beings and material objects no longer extend a friendly hand to one another; the relationship has become confrontational."

If we are honest and admit climate change threatens the survival of our species, right now and not next decade or next century, and don't just turn away or accept the numbing banality that comes with avoidance of the subject, we would have to, to not be hypocritical, actually choose to do something about what we know we know.

But do what, exactly? Our institutions are not working. Any real change has to come from our personal footprint, changing our choices. Change is our only way of being truthful with ourselves, and not neurotic or schizophrenic.

What is needed, says Margaret Klein Salamon, founder of Climate Change Mobilization, are achievable goals, a set of actions that anyone can take and appreciate that they are actually changing the situation for the better. Merely changing light bulbs or buying a Prius won't cut it. It has to involve not *green* consumerism but *de-consumerism*. We have to give up those fabulous perks that came with the Age of Oil; to discard zombie fashion. We have to stop having so many babies, eating so much meat, and cutting down so many trees. We have to go back to understanding our relationship with the land and our sources of sustenance, and showing greater care for the whole of the natural world that underpins our existence.

Salaman says:

> When people become agents for truth and vital change,
> they are elevated, enlarged, and lit up. The truth, and their
> role in advancing it, affects how they view themselves,
> what occupies their mind, and how they conduct their
> affairs. The power of truth allows them to transcend their
> limitations and what they once thought possible for
> themselves.

I cannot begin to say how refreshing it is to see Pope
Francis face the urgency of the situation and awaken us to
our need to be alive, and to swim upstream. In his new
encyclical, *Laudato Si',* [30]Francis writes:

> The violence present in our hearts, wounded by sin, is also
> reflected in the symptoms of sickness evident in the soil, in
> the water, in the air and in all forms of life. This is why the
> earth herself, burdened and laid waste, is among the most
> abandoned and maltreated of our poor; she "groans in
> travail" (Rom 8:22). We have forgotten that we ourselves
> are dust of the earth (cf. Gen 2:7); our very bodies are made
> up of her elements, we breathe her air and we receive life
> and refreshment from her waters.

***

> [I]f we no longer speak the language of fraternity and
> beauty in our relationship with the world, our attitude will
> be that of masters, consumers, ruthless exploiters, unable
> to set limits on their immediate needs. By contrast, if we
> feel intimately united with all that exists, then sobriety and
> care will well up spontaneously.

---

[30] laudatosi.com

The Pope comes out against technological advances that will save us from our modern sins or magically improve productivity by replacing human work. He eschews market-based mechanisms to solve environmental problems, condemning, like the popes before him, the profit motive at its root.

The New York Times columnist David Brooks, defender of both profits and the fossil economy, responds:

> Within marriage, lust can lead to childbearing. Within a regulated market, greed can lead to entrepreneurship and economic innovation. Within a constitution, the desire for fame can lead to political greatness.... [G]as and oil resources extracted through fracking have already added more than $430 billion to annual gross domestic product and supported more than 2.7 million jobs that pay, on average, twice the median US salary.

I won't quibble with either Brooks or the Pope because they are speaking past each other. Brooks is right that lust and greed are powerful motivators, and part of our serpent brain. Francis is right that to live at peace with each other and the planet we have to set aside those childish things, open our hearts, and begin to see the world as adults. Brooks is clinging to the past while Francis is salvaging the future.

Jeb Bush, shortly after announcing his candidacy for the US Presidency told a reporter about the Pope's statement, "I don't get my economic advice from my priest." His pollsters are telling him he is on the wrong side of the climate issue, but his strategists tell him he doesn't want to see the Koch brothers' billions go to a rival. Perhaps he thinks he will pivot later in the race, before he has to debate Bernie.

What is new is that it is not even about pandering to voters anymore. Even half of Republicans now want this issue dealt with. Well, good luck, because the zombie lies aren't about the voters. They're for the donors, who make their living killing the planet. The question is not *why* today's politicians suck more than ever, it is *who* they are sucking more than ever.

- Bill Maher

Paradigms change. Jason Hickel, Martin Kirk, and Joe Brewer, co-authors of a London School of Economics comparison between the encyclical and the UN's Sustainable Development Goals (SDGs), wrote in *The Guardian:* [31]

He calls out the transnational corporations that profit by polluting poor countries. He criticizes the foreign debt system that has become a tool by which rich countries control poor countries. And he warns that the financial sector, grown too powerful, has eroded the sovereignty of nation states and "tends to prevail over the political."

This is an important move, because without naming the forces that cause human suffering and environmental destruction, it is impossible to address them.

As Professor Ian Gough put it, "This revolutionary encyclical challenges both current ethics and economics."

Francis continues:

The basic problem goes even deeper: it is the way that humanity has taken up technology and its development according to an undifferentiated and one-dimensional

---

[31] theguardian.com/global-development-professionals-network/2015/jun/23/the- pope-united-nations-encyclical-sdgs

paradigm. This paradigm exalts the concept of a subject who, using logical and rational procedures, progressively approaches and gains control over an external object. This subject makes every effort to establish the scientific and experimental method, which in itself is already a technique of possession, mastery and transformation. It is as if the subject were to find itself in the presence of something formless, completely open to manipulation.

Men and women have constantly intervened in nature, but for a long time this meant being in tune with and respecting the possibilities offered by the things themselves. It was a matter of receiving what nature itself allowed, as if from its own hand. Now, by contrast, we are the ones to lay our hands on things, attempting to extract everything possible from them while frequently ignoring or forgetting the reality in front of us. Human beings and material objects no longer extend a friendly hand to one another; the relationship has become confrontational. This has made it easy to accept the idea of infinite or unlimited growth, which proves so attractive to economists, financiers and experts in technology. It is based on the lie that there is an infinite supply of the earth's goods, and this leads to the planet being squeezed dry beyond every limit.

It is the false notion that "an infinite quantity of energy and resources are available, that it is possible to renew them quickly, and that the negative effects of the exploitation of the natural order can be easily absorbed" (quoting the Pontifical Council For Justice And Peace, Compendium of the Social Doctrine of the Church, at page 462).

Here Francis begins to sound more like the Dalai Lama. *Tibetan Yoga and Secret Doctrines* [32] says, "Cherish no

---

[32] *Tibetan Yoga and Secret Doctrines: Seven Books of Wisdom of the Great Path, According to the Late Lama Kazi Dawa-Samdup's English*

notion of separated individuality." Subject and Object are one. Man and Nature are one. Form and Formlessness are one. Mind and Buddha are one. The encyclical says:

> It cannot be emphasized enough how everything is interconnected. Time and space are not independent of one another, and not even atoms or subatomic particles can be considered in isolation. Just as the different aspects of the planet - physical, chemical and biological - are interrelated, so too living species are part of a network, which we will never fully explore and understand. A good part of our genetic code is shared by many living beings. It follows that the fragmentation of knowledge and the isolation of bits of information can actually become a form of ignorance, unless they are integrated into a broader vision of reality.

Speaking directly to his "cheerfully reckless" critics, Francis says:

> It has become countercultural to choose a lifestyle whose goals are even partly independent of technology, of its costs and its power to globalize and make us all the same. Technology tends to absorb everything into its ironclad logic, and those who are surrounded with technology "know full well that it moves forward in the final analysis neither for profit nor for the well-being of the human race", that "in the most radical sense of the term power is its motive - a lordship over all" (quoting Omano Guardini, *Das Ende der Neuzeit* [The End of the Modern World]).

***

Rendering 3rd Edition by W. Y. Evans-Wentz (Author), Donald S. Lopez Jr.

Many things have to change course, but it is we human beings above all who need to change. We lack an awareness of our common origin, of our mutual belonging, and of a future to be shared with everyone. This basic awareness would enable the development of new convictions, attitudes and forms of life. A great cultural, spiritual and educational challenge stands before us, and it will demand that we set out on the long path of renewal.

The study by Hickel, Kirk, and Brewer contrasted Francis's vision with the UN's Sustainable Development Goals:

The SDGs are right to embrace a wide range of issues. Unlike their predecessors, the millennium development goals, they recognize that the problems we face are multidimensional. But they have confused thoroughness with holism, lists with patterns. It's a mistake born of outdated thinking.

The Pope, by contrast, has struck at the systemic nature of the issue. "It cannot be emphasized enough how everything is connected," he says. "To seek only a technical remedy to each environmental problem which comes up is to separate what is in reality interconnected and to mask the true and deepest problems of the global system."

This is what makes the encyclical far more than a document about climate change. It is a profound critique of the deep logic of our political economy. This is a vastly more sophisticated paradigm than the one that underpins the SDGs and a large part of why the encyclical feels cohesive, fresh and relevant, where the SDGs feel inconsistent, clunky and 20 years out of date.

Francis is not above legitimate criticism, less for what he puts into the encyclical than for what he leaves out.

Physicist Lawrence Krauss, writing for the *Bulletin of the Atomic Scientists*, says:

> First off, he dismisses the need to address reproductive rights for women, and also the concomitant problem of population growth in poor countries as part of any proposed solution to world environmental problems. If one is seriously worried about the environment on a global scale, then one needs to worry about population growth. A population of 10 billion by 2050 will likely be unsustainable at a level that provides all humans with adequate food and access to medicine, water, and security. Moreover, the environmental problems induced by overpopulation are also disproportionately borne by those in poor countries, where access to birth control and abortion is often limited. As I have argued elsewhere recently in this regard, ultimately empowering women to manage their own reproductive future gives them the surest road out of poverty.

Perhaps even more glaring is the double standard within which Francis, with Franciscan modesty, lives in a grand gilded palace, overseeing a legion of wealthy Cardinals, while calling for even the poorest among us to reduce consumption. To be sure, the encyclical was directed to believers within the church, including collegially off-key voices within the Vatican. Cardinal George Pell, its head of finance, currently immersed in a scandal involving pedophile priests in Australia, is a prominent climate change denier, and plenty of other senior Catholics are dredging up lame, discredited arguments against His Holiness's views. To them, Francis says:

> Christian spirituality proposes an alternative understanding of the quality of life, and encourages a prophetic and contemplative lifestyle, one capable of deep

enjoyment free of the obsession with consumption. We need to take up an ancient lesson, found in different religious traditions and also in the Bible. It is the conviction that "less is more". A constant flood of new consumer goods can baffle the heart and prevent us from cherishing each thing and each moment. To be serenely present to each reality, however small it may be, opens us to much greater horizons of understanding and personal fulfillment. Christian spirituality proposes a growth marked by moderation and the capacity to be happy with little. It is a return to that simplicity which allows us to stop and appreciate the small things, to be grateful for the opportunities which life affords us, to be spiritually detached from what we possess, and not to succumb to sadness for what we lack. This implies avoiding the dynamic of dominion and the mere accumulation of pleasures.

In 1978, Václav Havel, who led the non-violent Velvet Revolution and later became president of post-Soviet Czechoslovakia, wrote:

(The power of truth) does not reside in the strength of definable political or social groups, but chiefly in a potential, which is hidden throughout the whole of society, including the official power structures of that society. Therefore this power does not rely on soldiers of its own, but on soldiers of the enemy as it were - that is to say, on everyone who is living within the lie and who may be struck at any moment (in theory, at least) by the force of truth (or who, out of an instinctive desire to protect their position, may at least adapt to that force). It is a bacteriological weapon, so to speak, utilized when conditions are ripe by a single civilian to disarm an entire division.... This, too, is why the regime prosecutes, almost as a reflex action, preventatively, even modest attempts to live in truth.

Margaret Klein Salaman wrote, "Climate truth has the potential to be more powerful than any country's independence; more powerful than overthrowing authoritarian states; and more powerful than civil rights or any group's struggle for safety, recognition and equality. Climate truth contains such superordinate power because all of those causes depend on a safe climate."

Will the Papal Encyclical make any real difference in the battle against climate change? One need only recall what happened in 1979, when John Paul II traveled to Poland and preached thirty-two sermons in nine days. Timothy Garton Ash[33] put it this way, "Without the Pope, no Solidarity. Without Solidarity, no Gorbachev. Without Gorbachev, no fall of communism." Bogdan Szajkowski [34]said it was "a psychological earthquake, an opportunity for mass political catharsis...." The Poles who turned out by the millions looked around and saw they were not alone.

---

[33] Timothy Garton Ash CMG FRSA is a British historian, author and commentator. He is Professor of European Studies at Oxford University.
[34] Bogdan Szajkowski., author: Comparative Politics, European Politics, Asian Politics. Author of *Marxist Local Governments in Western Europe and Japan.*

The Gift of the Maya

"The Maya forest garden holds, in its ramblings and roots, a hidden-in-plain-sight way through our present crises."

It takes a bit of time for the elegance of a food forest to emerge, something on the order of decades. Strolling the garden through the morning mist in a hot Tennessee summer, we tried to remember what this landscape looked like 21 years ago, when we moved to this site, set up our yurt, and started in on our little corner of paradise.

What we see today does not remotely resemble what was here then. Then there was a wire-fenced, stony horse paddock in a re-emerging poplar forest. The deep soil tilth now is blanketed in thick vines; their giant leaves hiding pumpkins, squashes, and melons. Bamboo cathedrals twined with akebia and passionfruit arch 70 feet (20 meters) over a duck pond next to our cob henhouse. As we let out our poultry for their daily bug chase, bullfrogs croak and leap away. A snapping turtle submerges beneath the mat of duckweed and hyacinths at the water's edge. All around us figs, peaches, apples, pears, blueberries, cranberries, cherries, plums, and persimmons bend down boughs under the weight of their fruit, rabbits stealing out to grab a windfall and then hop back to cover, while high up in the oaks, beech, butternuts, and hickories, squirrel forest wardens check the progress of their winter larder.

All this complexity, shrouded in mist and glistening in dew, would not be called orderly by farmers trained in Ag schools or raised in a tradition of straight rows and powerful machines with air-conditioned cabs. They can pump food from the earth the way you would pump barrels of oil, but not without depleting reserves accumulated over eons. As they pour on chemicals, the genetically monocultured crops gradually but inexorably lose nutrient density and attract predators.

Our general health as a society reflects that loss and malaise. Family treasures are squandered on biotech voodoo and Roundup potions in the pursuit of a false paradigm of technological progress, but the escalating fixes are unable to stem the tide of biological entropy. And all the while, just beyond the fences, magical weeds of awesome power dance in anticipation of the invaders' surrender and patiently await the return of their lost domain.

We have been reading *The Maya Forest Garden* by Anabel Ford and Ronald Nigh. It tells the tale of a civilization that weathered many climate changes, foreign conquests, and failed attempts at cultural genocide. That civilization is still there today, after 8,000 years. There are more children born and raised in families today whose first language is a Mayan dialect than during the Classic period 1400 years ago.

When the first two-leggeds arrived in Mesoamerica over 10,000 years ago, the region was cool and arid - akin to the Great Plains of central Canada. Over the next 2,000 years, as the Hemisphere continued to emerge from the great Ice Age, Mesoamerica became a warm and wet tropical region, reaching an early heating peak during the Holocene Thermal Maximum before settling back to the wet tropics we find there today.

Ford and Nigh disagree with popular myths told by historians of rapacious city-states that denuded their landscape to bake lime for painting temples and then starved. They write:

> The Maya and their ancestors have been living in this region for more than 10,000 years. Why would they cut down the forest that was their garden? Even after concerted efforts by governments and private interests to convert forest to pasture over the past half of the twentieth century, and after development schemes to introduce commercial annual monocrops into the perennial polycultivated croplands, and in spite of global trade agreements that have jeopardized the smallholder, the Maya forest has lived to tell the tale.

***

> It is important to understand that the developed European culture views agriculture and forests as incompatible. That idea is embedded in our understanding of "arable" [Latin: to plow] and in the Malthusian view that agricultural lands are finite, based on the medieval concept of "assart," the act of converting forest into arable land.

***

> To evaluate ancient land use, we must conjure a world without the plow, without cattle or horses, where work in the fields was accomplished by hand, and where transport was on foot.

According to Ford and Nigh, the Maya forest garden was not just an indelible feature that withstood the rise and fall of successive empires, but holds, in its ramblings and roots, a hidden-in-plain-sight way through our present crises.

We argue that conservation of the Maya forest must engage the traditional farmer, whose skills and knowledge created - and continue to maintain - the forest and its culture.

Land use changed over time based on social constraints. In ancient times, smallholders who produced a variety of goods and services from the forest were at times compelled to increase production to pay taxes and to feed the elites and their armies. This process continues today. Greater demands for exports from the forest require denser populations, because working hilly terrain without machines or animals requires hands and feet. Today it may imply imported labor, a form of economic slavery not much different than in the Classic Maya era. To the extent that human labor for cultivation and transportation has been replaced with fossil energy, the requirements for human slaves have diminished.

One barrel of oil has 5.7 million BTUs of energy, or 1700 kWh. An average adult can, in hard labor, generate 0.6 kWh/day. That's 11 years of human labor packed into each barrel of oil. Put another way, fifty dollars currently buys you eleven petroleum slaves working year-round at hard labor. What would those slaves cost if they were human? Ten thousand dollars? Half a million dollars? It depends on where you get them and what tasks they perform for you.

Thanks to petroslavery, we have higher wages, higher profits, really cheap products, and more people doing little to nothing. The average USAnian uses 60 barrels per year (or equivalent coal, gasoline, and fracked gas) or roughly 660 fossil slaves standing at the beck and call of each and every citizen. Those numbers are quite a bit less in the Mayan world today, but nonetheless significant, and growing. Farmers don't have to carry corn and mangoes to the city on their backs, although no one has yet found a way to machine-harvest cacao or spray-pollinate vanilla vines.

Nonetheless, extraction costs for fossil fuels are rising - 17% per year for the past 10 years. That drives up energy costs and as that price goes up, it's like having to pay your slaves. Profits decline, and some slaves get laid off.

As we lose our energy slaves, will we go back to sending our army to snatch human slaves from weaker or less militaristic neighbors? The Classic Maya were something like that. With cheap slave energy gained by conquest, they paved roads and built pyramids. Many historians assume they overran their resources or had a slave revolt, but Ford and Nigh have eliminated ecocide, because food resources never diminished. Slavery has its limits and the Maya's slaves may have reached theirs.

Misleading assumptions about Mayan ecological demise, and climate over 10,000 years, came from paleoclimatic reconstructions based on lake sediments and pollen counts. Ford and Nigh point out that the pollen data emphasize windborne pollen, and yet, in the tropics, all but about 2 percent of plants are pollinated by bees, birds, bats, and butterflies.

Ford and Nigh picked up clues from ramón[35] trees and grassland forbs,[36] which were better indicators of the milpa

---

[35] The ramón tree stretches to heights of more than 120 feet and produces a nut that provides nutrition comparable to maize.
[36] A forb (sometimes spelled phorb) is a herbaceous flowering plant that is not a graminoid (grasses, sedges and rushes).

cycle.[37] While climate perturbations, sometimes severe, occurred repeatedly, the heaviest climate changes came in the Early Holocene,[38] before the appearance of the Maya. The milpa system evolved in that era, as proof of concept for climate-resilient agriculture.

> The Maya resource system, based on the milpa forest garden cycle of the past and present, adapts to extreme conditions by moderating the impacts of deluges and managing land cover against drought. The system was resilient under conditions of change, and the climatic stability of the Classic Era promoted the rise of the Maya civilization.

Ford and Nigh conclude that the Classic Era, while it was not without impact - evidenced by high phosphorus lake sediment loading and diminishing soil quality - did not end from an environmental collapse. And yet, 1100 years ago, the Empire broke down and retreated back into the jungle. Civic centers gradually depopulated and rural farms resumed their ubiquity. Soil quality began to improve and runoff to decrease.

The Maya did not disappear, they dispersed. Having little to interest outside invaders, the last of their strongholds, at Nojpeten, was not conquered by the Spanish until 1697, on the Ides of March. (In ancient Greece, that date also marked *Pharmakos*, which involved beating an old man dressed in animal skins and driving him from the city. History may not repeat, but it rhymes.)

---

[37] The milpa cycle calls for clearing, followed by a short period of cultivation for annual crops and a longer period for cultivation of forest perennials.

[38] The early Holocene began about 12,000 years before present.

When the human slavery system ended, it was not replaced by machine or animal slaves (they had neither). It was replaced with tree crops - vegetable slaves - toiling without complaint, providing myriad household and ecological services, and asking only the occasional tender loving care. Skills that could glean the most from any terrain were passed generation to generation down to the present.

In the Cartesian view of the world everything is separated into chemicals, physical properties, or energy systems. The quantum entanglement of the real world is much less simple. It took a few thousand years for humans to find harmony with their environment and to co-evolve the comfortable Holocene climate, as much a product of human respect for the limits of the natural world as of galactic and planetary cycles. No doubt some shaman warned a Neolithic hunting party not to slay the last mastodon, but they didn't listen, and we got an Ice Age, or worse, agriculture.

Once the original instructions were forgotten, thanks in no small measure to electric lights, television, and the internet, the Holocene weave began unraveling. Biodiversity and soil fertility plummeted, population skyrocketed, and the popular culture of idle elite tilted to the kinky, bloodthirsty, and perverse. If this sounds like the Maya, that would not be far wrong, but we are speaking of the times we live in. We have lost our way.

The Maya forest shows us a way home, should we choose to take it.

This past Thursday, NASA senior scientist James Hansen and 17 co-authors published a paper, "Ice melt, sea level rise and superstorms: evidence from paleoclimate data, climate modeling, and modern observations that 2°C global warming is highly dangerous," in the Atmospheric Chemistry and Physics discussion group.[39] The paper noted that despite repeated warnings for more than 25 years, global greenhouse gas emissions continue to increase and fossil fuels remain the primary energy source.

"The argument is made that it is economically and morally responsible to continue fossil fuel use for the sake of raising living standards, with expectation that humanity can adapt to climate change and find ways to minimize effects via advanced technologies," the paper says. "We suggest that a strategic approach relying on adaptation to such consequences is unacceptable to most of humanity...."

Specifically, the authors, making an end run around lengthy peer review in order to address delegates who will gather at the UN climate summit in Paris in December, point out that even if the UN denouement is extraordinarily successful and achieves its 2-degree target, civilization will not avert catastrophe.

As Natalia Shakhova, a professor at the University of Alaska Fairbanks, told Dahr Jamail of Truthout[40] last January, the transition from the methane being frozen in the permafrost, either on land or in the shallow continental shelves, "is not gradual. When it comes to phase transition, it appears to be a relatively short, jump-like transformation from one state of the process to another state. The difference between the two states is like the difference between a closed valve and an open valve. This kind of a

[39] csas.ei.columbia.edu/2015/07/23/ice-melt-sea-level-rise-and-superstorms/
[40] truth-out.org/news/item/28490-the-methane-monster-roars

release is like the unsealing of an over-pressurized pipeline."

Shakhova has been warning for years that a 50-gigaton "burp" of methane from thawing Arctic permafrost beneath the East Siberian sea is "highly possible at any time." That would be the equivalent of 1,000 gigatons of carbon dioxide ($GtCO_2$), three thousand times what is released from the Siberian shelf in an average year, and the amount that the IPCC Fifth Assessment (2013) said was the carbon budget for all anthropogenic releases this century if we want to hold warming to 2°C. Humans have released approximately 1,475 $GtCO_2$ since 1850 from fossil fuel burning and land use changes. The ocean absorbed 90 percent of that, some frozen in ocean sediments as clathrates. [41]

The Permian mass extinction of approximately 95 percent of all species on the planet 250 million years ago was triggered by a massive lava flow in an area of Siberia that led to an increase in global temperatures of 6 degrees Celsius. The lava caused the melting of frozen methane deposits under the seas. Released into the atmosphere, the Permian methane "burp" caused temperatures to skyrocket.

Hansen's group warns that is not too late to avert a similar fate this time, but it will take more than reducing carbon emissions.

> Rapid transition to abundant affordable carbon-free electricity is the core requirement, as that would also permit production of net-zero-carbon liquid fuels from electricity. The rate at which CO_2 emissions must be

---

[41] A clathrate is a chemical lattice that traps or contains molecules of frozen gas, typically methane.

reduced is about 6%/yr to reach 350 ppm atmospheric CO_2 by about 2100, under the assumption that improved agricultural and forestry practices could sequester 100 GtC.

Actually, we know that improved agricultural and forestry practices can sequester on the order of 10 GtC annually, and could return the atmosphere and oceans to pre-industrial greenhouse chemistries (250 ppmv CO_2e) by 2100 if scaled rapidly. We know that from studying, among other clues, the Maya forest.

Ford and Nigh conclude:

> If we take these real human and ecological costs into account and systematically compare them to the intensive Maya milpa, we find that milpa is neither primitive nor unproductive and is positive for human health and the environment. Food produced by the milpa is of high quality, as it is based on the natural fertility maintained in the forest garden cycle, where regenerated woodlands continually restore minerals and organic matter. High biodiversity assures that pesticides are unnecessary and all wastes are recycled in the field. Water is managed by the conservation of vegetation and by the infiltration of rainwater stored in the soil. A healthy and natural relationship is fostered for animals that are attracted to the secondary vegetation of the milpa forest garden, resulting in a kind of semi-domestication based on the landscape. Dependence on fossil fuels is nonexistent, and far from contributing to greenhouse gas emissions, the Maya milpa creates a long-term store of carbon in the soil.
>
> Significantly, the milpa and its diversity provide a livelihood for farm families and a food surplus for local markets.

***

Yet milpa agroforestry seems to violate the master narrative of our times: the incessant march of progress from hunter-gatherer to complex sedentary agriculture. The Eurocentric vision assumes that Western civilization is the pinnacle of human progress and that disappearing cultures can only aspire to emulate it. Not only in the popular mind but also in the view of scientists, politicians, and technicians, it is capitalist industrial agriculture that is the unquestioned standard of production; all previously existing forms are, in this view, ready to be replaced.

We must vindicate the milpa forest garden and similarly sophisticated systems of human ecology that are native to their place. Their intricacy, subtlety, and contribution to our environmental balances are critical to our future.

The gift of the Maya, at least some of them, is to never have forgotten. The gift of Anabel Ford and Ronald Nigh, and James Hansen, after rigorous lifetimes in this arcane scientific pursuit, is the retelling of that story to a world audience.

Sunday, August 2, 2015

Mysteries of Eleuthera

"What kind of force can leave a four million pound rock on top of a cliff? According to the oceanographers, it was waves."

The Glass Window Bridge of North Eleuthera[42] is one of the island's more popular attractions. Once a naturally formed bridge of rock, it was destroyed in a hurricane and has been replaced by a man-made version, presently in need of repair. From the bridge, a narrow span uniting separated parts of the long, thin island, you can see the dark blue Atlantic churning away to the east and the calm turquoise waters of the Caribbean to the west.

In their seminal piece on the emerging Hyper-Anthropocene, James Hansen and co-authors provide a photo of mysterious boulders on a cliff overlooking the Atlantic Ocean. The boulders, we now know after extensive research by many geological experts, were dredged from the ocean floor, taken up and over a cliff and left there like Easter Island statuary, in a great storm event during a past interglacial warming epoch. The largest weighs about 2300 tons.

It is hard to imagine that the air we exhale lifted these huge boulders, but indirectly, it did. "CO_2 is the principal determinant of Earth's climate state, the 'control knob' that sets global mean temperature," Hansen's group says, pointing to the ice core correlations between temperature and CO_2 tracing in lockstep back 800,000 years. CO_2, once

---

[42] Eleuthera is an island in the Bahamas, lying 50 miles (80 km) east of Nassau.

emitted, takes 100,000 years to be removed from the atmosphere by nature.

> To provide a comfortable climate for mammals such as ourselves, atmospheric concentrations of 260 ppm CO_2 prevailed through much of the Holocene, a far cry from the Anthropocene's current 400 and rising.

> The CO_2 dial must be turned to □ 260 ppm to achieve a Holocene-level interglacial. CO_2 □ 250 ppm was sufficient for quasi-interglacials in the period 800-450,000 years before present, with sea level 10-25 m lower than in the Holocene. Interglacials with CO_2 [at]□ 280 ppm, i.e., the Eemian and Holsteinian (400,000 years ago), were warmer than the Holocene and had sea level at least several meters higher than today.

For many years, climate scientists have predicted that sea level rise would be slow but inexorable, driven less by ice melt and more by thermal expansion of water molecules. Because of the speed with which humans are changing climate, this conventional wisdom has been undermined. Newer science shows that the paleohistoric[43] sea level changed not over 1000-year periods, as earlier thought, but in decades to centuries.

The IPCC (2013) report increased estimates of sea level rise compared to prior IPCC reports, but scenarios they discuss are close to linear responses to the assumed rising climate forcing. The most extreme climate forcing [RCP8.5, 936 ppm CO_2 in 2100] is estimated to produce 0.74 m sea level rise in 2100 relative to the 1986-2005 mean sea level, with the "likely" range of uncertainty 0.52-0.98 m.

---

[43] Paleohistory is the study of the physical remains of ancient cultures or eras.

Less than a meter rise over the coming 85 years is no longer credible. The reason is the rate of ice melt. Ice melt is proceeding so fast now that it will be the primary driver of sea level rise this century. Moreover, what is being added to the oceans, primarily at the poles, is freshwater, not saltwater. Freshwater sinks at a different rate than saltwater, so in those parts of the Earth where there is a downwelling of the oceans, the current will be slowed. For the Atlantic Conveyor, this slowing effect has not yet been confirmed by observations. Nevertheless, Hansen's models predict a 30% slowdown by 2100. As the driving currents that move oceans around the world slow, heat becomes more concentrated at the Equator. The differential is magnified by the cooling effect of ice water pouring into the oceans at the poles.

Sea level rise will occur rapidly at high latitudes because of ice melt. Sea level rise will also occur at low latitudes, but because of more profound thermal expansion there.

But there is another, bigger impact in the tropics, and it involves those Eleutherian boulders. Ocean warming will disturb familiar weather patterns.

Owing to the spin of the Earth and the equatorial heat of the land surface in Africa, tropical depressions typically emerge every three or four days off the west coast of Africa and then drift west within the trade winds across the Atlantic Ocean.. As they reach the warmer waters of the continental shelf, they pick up strength. More available heat energy builds bigger hurricanes.

What kind of force can leave a four-million-pound rock on top of a cliff? According to the oceanographers, it was ocean waves, propelled by "a potent sustained energy source" taken from an unusually warm tropical ocean and strong zonal temperature gradients in the North Atlantic. These conditions last existed at the end of the Eemian epoch, before the last great ice age, 115-120 thousand years ago.

Hansen writes:

> The boulders must have been transported to their present position by waves, as two of the largest ones are located on the crest of the island's ridge, eliminating the possibility that they were moved downward by gravity or are the karstic[44] remnants of some ancient landscape. A tsunami conceivably could have deposited the boulders, but the area is not near a tectonic plate boundary. The coincidence of a tsunami at the end-Eemian moment is improbable given the absence of evidence of tsunamis at other times in the Bahamas and the lack of evidence of tsunamis on the Atlantic Coastal Plain of the United States. The proximity of run-up deposits and nested chevron ridges across a broad front of Bahamian islands is clear evidence of a sustained series of high-energy wave events.

Sea level rise relative to coastlines is not gradual. Storms are the means by which changes occur, because in their scale and violence they carve new landscapes that remain altered when the events subside. New bays are formed, old ones filled in. Barrier islands are erased, peninsulas split into islands, and cliffs are carved from windward slopes.

> Temperature change in 2065, 2080 and 2096 for 10 year doubling time should be thought of as results when sea level rise reaches 0.6, 1.7 and 5 m, because the dates depend on initial freshwater flux. Actual current freshwater flux

---

[44] Karst topography is a landscape formed from the dissolution of soluble rocks such as limestone, dolomite, and gypsum.

may be about a factor of four higher than assumed in these initial runs, as we will discuss, and thus effects may occur 20 years earlier. A sea level rise of 5 m [16 feet] in a century is about the most extreme in the paleo record but the assumed 21st century climate forcing is also more rapidly growing than any known natural forcing. [45]

Another effect of the freshwater is to retard the speed of ocean warming, since salt stores heat more efficiently than water. This is good news in the near term, but worrisome once the freshwater input ends, about the same time sea level rise reaches 5 meters. Then the cooling effect is removed and the full effect of warming begins to be felt. The oceans warm much faster, the energy imparted to storms becomes much greater, and besides the pounding surf, we may once more experience boulders the size of Volkswagens being deposited miles inland.

Of course, it will be a wonder if anyone is still there then. Yesterday the heat recorded in the city of Bandar Mahshahr, Southern Iran, was 115°F, but when you add the moisture - the dew point was 90 - it felt like 165 (74°C). Will this be coming soon to a place near you? The best scientific minds seem to think so.

Team Hansen says:

> [T]here is no morally defensible excuse to delay phase-out of fossil fuel emissions as rapidly as possible. We conclude that the 2°C global warming "guardrail", affirmed in the Copenhagen Accord (2009), does not provide safety, as

---

[45] A climate forcing is any influence on climate that originates from outside the climate system itself. The climate system includes the oceans, land surface, cryosphere, biosphere, and atmosphere. Examples of external forcings include: solar activity, surface reflectivity (albedo) and human induced changes in greenhouse gases.

such warming would likely yield sea level rise of several meters along with numerous other severely disruptive consequences for human society and ecosystems .... Given the inertia of the climate and energy systems, and the grave threat posed by continued high emissions, the matter is urgent and calls for emergency cooperation among nations.

Sunday, August 9, 2015

Snatching Defeat

"What we must ask is what we intend to sustain when we speak of sustainability?"

We concluded our last chapter on climate change with a quote from James Hansen, "The matter is urgent and calls for emergency cooperation among nations." All this year we have been leading up to our collective *fin-de-siècle* moment in December, the grand denouement of the Framework Convention on Climate Change and Kyoto Protocol in Paris. At this late date, I am frankly pessimistic for the outcome there.

It isn't that I expect the parchment won't get inked, but rather that the document won't actually accomplish its task even if the conference is a complete success. After more than two decades of negotiating for every paragraph, the Paris Treaty will be two decades out of date and strategically misdirected.

In those 20 years, the goalposts have moved. They are not farther away now. They are closer.

The United Nations, Eleanor Roosevelt's singular passion, is showing signs of age, architecturally symbolized by its under-maintained (owing to deadbeat nations who never pay their dues, nudge to the ribs of USAnians) 1950s rusting steel and chipped glass edifice fronting the East River on the New York skyline. Instead of peering through the mists into a bright but challenging future, the building peers out across the river to Roosevelt Island and back in time to a Rooseveltian utopia with strong labor unions and a chicken in every pot.

Actually, a-chicken-in-every-pot was the 1928 campaign slogan of Herbert Hoover, a Republican president who presided over the Crash of '29. Hoover advocated "kinder, gentler" capitalism. He said, "We want to see a nation built of homeowners and farm owners. We want to see more and more of them insured against death and accident, unemployment and old age." It would become the mantra of future candidates of both parties, a code for enslaving the working class through health and home insurance, college and mortgage loans, while feathering the nests of banks and insurance companies.

This is oddly where we find the United Nations now, making impossible promises to lure the gullible while holding a finger on the scales of justice.

Like a military bureaucracy busily arming with the obsolete weapons of the last war, the United Nations is stuck in the past century, driving a pink Cadillac to the mall. Here, for instance, is a chart of its projections for world population, which it derives from fertility, life expectancy, and demographic trends over the past decades:

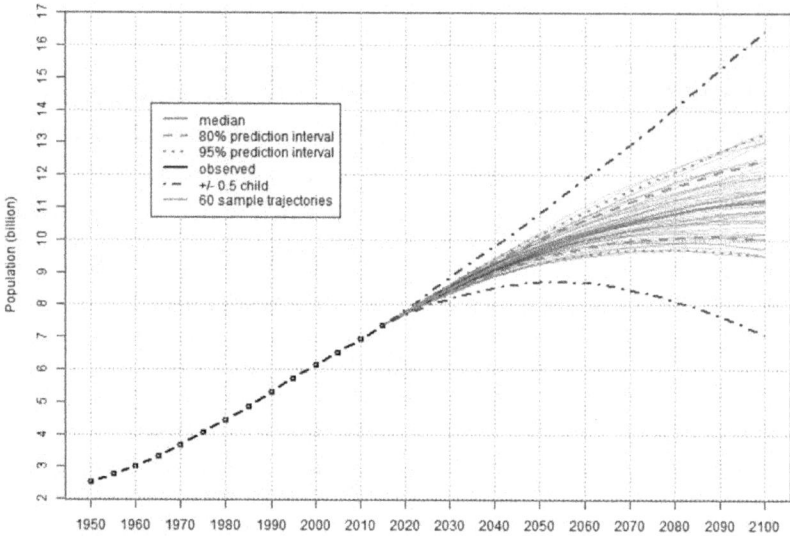

WORLD: Total Population

Those dash-dotted blue lines at the margins are the range that would be accomplished if there were half-a-child more or fewer births per woman than at present. Half-a-child smaller families is all it would take to move planetary stress out of the red zone.

Another way would be for the entire globe to follow the example of Greece and depopulate immediately, just by starving pensioners and slashing budgets for hospitals, fire departments, and other vital services.

One problem is that projecting the past into the future is always a fool's errand. Consider the UN's projections for low-lying island nations:

Marshall Islands: Total Population

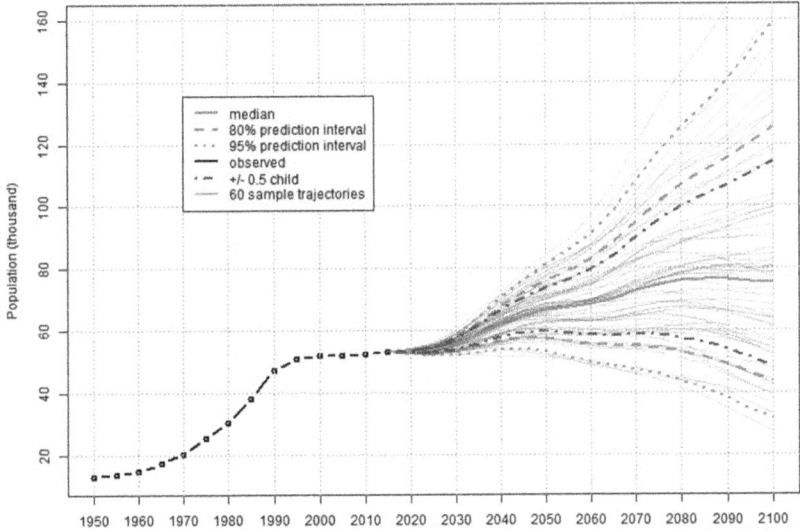

By 2100, if not 2050, most of these low-lying chains will be under the ocean. Are these projected people still worth counting if by century's end they can be presumed to be in refugee camps, waiting at border crossings in places like Calais, or in submarine cities?

Which brings us back to stranded expectations.

Our friend Joe Brewer,[46] a linguist who, with George Lakoff[47] and others, developed the concept of "framing," wrote a thoughtful piece on the language of the UN's sustainable development goals, now scheduled for ratification in September. Just take a moment, though, to consider the embodied ignorance of a term like "sustainable development."

---

[46] Joe Brewer is a social entrepreneur and cognitive scientist.
[47] Lakoff is an American cognitive linguist, best known for his thesis that lives of individuals are significantly influenced by the central metaphors they use to explain complex phenomena.

What is it, exactly, that we wish to sustain? Development? What kind? Do we want Donald Trump to build condos for billionaires in Namibia? Or maybe we want more jobs for Namibians assembling smartphones in Chinese factories while former Chinese factory slaves spend their renminbi vacationing in Dubai? Last month the long laboring UN Open Working Group announced it had formalized 17 Sustainable Development Goals with 169 associated targets and deemed them "integrated and indivisible." It submitted a lengthy report for ratification by the 69th Session of the UN General Assembly in September. Beaming with pride at its accomplishment, it bragged:

> Never before have world leaders pledged common action and endeavor across such a broad and universal policy agenda. We are setting out together on the path towards sustainable development, devoting ourselves collectively to the pursuit of global development and of "win-win" cooperation which can bring huge gains to all countries and all parts of the world.

And then, in the next breath, it snatched defeat from the jaws of victory: "We reiterate that every state has, and shall freely exercise, full permanent sovereignty over its wealth and natural resources."

> We will implement the Agenda for the full benefit of all, for today's generation and for future generations. In doing so, we reaffirm our commitment to international law and emphasize that the Agenda is to be implemented in a manner that is consistent with the rights and obligations of states under international law, taking into account different national circumstances, capacities and priorities.

With these caveats, the UN essentially emasculated its own achievement. It was kind of like saying, "From now on, no one shall be allowed to shoot heroin or smoke crack. We will accomplish this through voluntary self-regulation by all would-be addicts."

The simile is not that far-fetched. Neurobiologists and psychologists who have studied the problem of addiction have a much more nuanced picture of crime and punishment than do lawmakers or the public. They know what can reduce addiction - supportive community ties and self-respect, among other factors - and what elevates it - punishment, isolation and disgrace - but they have been unable to make that scientific case in public debate without getting shouted down, and so the criminal justice system stereotypes and victimizes addicts.

How the UN plans to discipline unfettered growth addicts is by loving them. Not tough love. Friendly advice kind of love. A forgive but not forget kind of love.

The UN plan continues:

> The new Goals and targets will come into effect on 1 January 2016 and will guide the decisions we take over the next fifteen years. All of us will work to implement the Agenda within our own countries and at the regional and global levels. We will at the same time take into account different national realities, including capacities and levels of development, and culture. We will respect national policies and priorities and policy space for economic growth, in particular for developing states, while remaining consistent with relevant international rules and commitments. We acknowledge also the importance of the regional and sub-regional dimensions, regional economic integration and interconnectivity in sustainable development. Regional and sub-regional frameworks can

facilitate the effective translation of sustainable development policies into concrete action at national level.

Brewer says:

The frame of national sovereignty conceals the much more nuanced picture of networked financial assets that are coordinated through a nested shell system of corporate structures - enabling things like the tax haven system and cross-cultural propaganda efforts that shape social norms at scales of regional markets.

The Committee on Sustainable Development:

We are committed to ending poverty in all its forms, including extreme poverty, by 2030. All people must enjoy a basic standard of living, including through social protection systems. We are also determined to end hunger and malnutrition and to achieve food security as a matter of priority. We will devote resources to developing rural areas and supporting small farmers, especially women farmers, herders and fishers.

***

We will seek to build strong economic foundations for all our countries. Sustained, inclusive and sustainable economic growth is essential for prosperity. This will only be possible if wealth is shared and income inequality is addressed. We will work to build dynamic, sustainable, innovative and people-centered economies, promoting youth employment and women's economic empowerment, in particular, and decent work for all. We will eradicate forced labor and human trafficking and eliminate all the worst forms of child labor. All countries stand to benefit from having a healthy and well-educated workforce with the knowledge and skills needed for productive and fulfilling work and full participation in society. We will adopt policies which increase productive capacities, productivity and productive employment; financial inclusion; sustainable agriculture, pastoralist and fisheries development; sustainable industrial development; universal access to affordable, reliable, sustainable and modern energy services; sustainable transport systems; and resilient infrastructure.

Lately I have been trying to purge my vocabulary of the word "sustainable" (as offensive to polar bears) in much the way I purged my vocabulary of "rule of thumb" 20 years ago (as offensive to women, even though the origin was a parody, not an actual law, that husbands could beat wives with canes no wider than a thumb).

What we must ask is what we intend to sustain when we speak of sustainability? Is it, as Iowa Congressman Paul Simon famously proclaimed, our God-given right to the American way of life? Is it exponential growth of resource consumption on a finite planet? Is it a sustained rate of whale kill, coal burning, or forest clearing? What are we talking about sustaining once fossil fuels no longer can give us all those billions of energy slaves?

As my friend Mark Robinowitz[48] told me:

> The Hansen approach - concentrating on a "we obviously want to continue western civilization, that's not the question" perspective, can be seen as a form of denial.

Joe Brewer, looking at the Sustainable Development Goals, unpacked four foundational weaknesses revealed by their language:

---

[48] peakchoice.org

Insight #1: The entire effort rests on a mis-framing of poverty. The SDG documents consistently frame poverty as a disease, which, in contrast to their own promise to eradicate it by 2030, evokes the logic that it should be expected and managed, but cannot go away. When they conceptualize poverty this way, they misunderstand what it is and overlook the essential list of structural causes that must be addressed for any transition to a sustainable world. They fail to say how poverty is created.

Insight #2: The language obscures "development as usual." It ignores this topic entirely and fails to articulate that it is based on a particular, specifically neoliberal and corporatist conception of how the world economy does and should work. Also noteworthy, there is no reference to corporations - the most powerful institutions on the planet, whose influence in development spaces has been growing considerably in recent years, including via this process - an omission that prompts suspicion that an unpopular agenda may sneak through under the radar. This has the effect of neutralizing analysis on the core elements of the development model, and any consideration for the role of power politics or financial influence in development outcomes.

Insight #3: The poison pill is growth; specifically undifferentiated, perpetual growth as represented by GDP as a measure of progress. An awareness is acknowledged of the deep problems and contradictions when relying on GDP growth to tackle poverty. It is then deliberately kicked into the long grass and left as the prime operative of economic development. Indeed, the only thing the SDG framework has to offer on this is that it has nothing meaningful to offer; instead it passes this challenge to future generations.

Insight #4: The language is self-contradictory and conflicted on the relationship between nature and the economy. There is a clear and laudable intent to connect development and the environment - indeed, calling themselves the Sustainable Development Goals they could not make a bigger signal about needing development to be sustainable - but then the logic repeatedly demonstrates a confused and contradictory understanding of whether the economy is something linked with or separate from nature; there to dominate or work within. No credible use of the word sustainable would perform this way.

These insights lead to a simple antidote that can heal the SDG process and move us closer to real sustainability - tell the story of poverty creation that reveals systemic and structural causes of "development as usual." Brewer's key point is that poverty is not a disease, something you catch by being born in the wrong place or choosing to be a slacker. Poverty is institutionally created. The rules of the system are set up to extract wealth from the economy and hoard it in the hands of the few who control the money supply. This is done through unfair trade agreements, regressive tax structures and tax evasion, structural debt relations, land grabs, privatization of public utilities, and other widely used business practices.

When the SDG framework conceptualizes poverty as a disease, it misunderstands what it is and overlooks this essential list of structural causes that must be addressed for any transition to a sustainable world. Part of the problem, Brewer suspects, is that we like to break large, unmanageable problems down into smaller, more manageable pieces. In this case, the UN is putting different issues - rights of women and children, indigenous peoples, unsustainable agriculture, deforestation and desertification, energy costs and climate change - into issue silos, rather than treating them as part of a larger pattern of our human relationship to nature. Brewer says the two competing systems - environment and development:

> ... are treated as separate and distinct, which artificially divides humans from nature - an untenable position that ignores the foundational knowledge of physics and biology for living systems.

He points out that mischaracterizing poverty as a disease leads to a complete disconnect when wealthy countries are confronted with the need to scale back or pay reparations - those countries that are "less developed" could be reframed as "more pillaged," and those that are "more developed" are countries that have "reaped the benefits of pillage" - and also when underdeveloping countries are told they should no longer try to imitate the West and think that some day they will be able to consume and hoard on a comparable scale. What enabled the wealthy nations to pillage was the presence of natural wealth - human, plant and mineral - that could be brought under the sword or cross and systematically extracted. Where now do emerging economies like China, Brazil, India, and South Korea turn to find such wealth? How does the aristocracy of the overdeveloped world keep its high-entropy investments secure without finding somewhere new to recharge them?

> The UN working group is silent on these points because it has accepted without challenge a Neoliberal world view and ignored the over-consumption, financial destabilization, and enlarging inequality that demands.

Australian rancher Darren Doherty[49] who has designed regenerative retrofits of more than 2000 mostly broadacre, permaculture landscapes and is author, with Andrew Jeeves, of *Regrarians Handbook,* is fond of saying that sustainability is a weak ambition to begin with. "You are treading water. Is that all you want to do, tread water?"

Kate Raworth[50] is a renegade economist teaching at Oxford University's Environmental Change Institute. She is currently writing *Doughnut Economics: Seven ways to think like a 21ˢᵗ century economist,* to be published by Random House in 2016. She looks at the issue of framing in the context of what the French call *decroissance,* "degrowth":

> The debates currently being had under the banner of degrowth are among the most important economic debates for the 21st century. But most people don't realize that because the name puts them off. We urgently need to articulate an alternative, positive vision of an economy in a way that is widely engaging. Here's the best way I have come up with so far to say it:
>
> We have an economy that needs to grow, whether or not it makes us thrive.
>
> We need an economy that makes us thrive, whether or not it grows.
>
> Is that "degrowth"? I don't actually know. But what I do know is that whenever I frame it like this in debates, lots of people nod, and the discussion soon moves on to identifying how we are currently locked into a must-grow economy - through the current design of government,

---

[49] www.regrarians.org.
[50] www.kateraworth.com

business, finance, and politics - and what it would take to free ourselves from that lock-in so that we can pursue social justice with ecological integrity instead.

We need to reframe this debate in a way that tempts many more people to get involved if we are ever to build the critical mass needed to change the dominant economic narrative.

Regeneration is a much more hopeful and ambitious term: Civilization 2.0. The goal is not to sustain high entropy habitation and extend it to 7 billion or 12 billion people, but to redesign habitation to be low-entropy and biodiverse, letting nature heal, and to gradually bring human numbers down to something that is more (watch out, almost said sustainable) manageable within ecosystemic limits.

A couple years ago the UN Commission on Human Rights issued a report to address the subject of whether provision of minimum food support is a human right. The only practical way that could be achieved without overexploiting all the available arable land, the report said, was by transition to what they termed "eco-agriculture" but was really permaculture - primarily tree-crops and perennial grasses with some aquaculture. As we described here last week, this approach is also much more adaptive and mitigating in the climate change context, as our ancestors discovered several thousand years ago.

I am training myself to use "resilience" and "regenerative" in place of "sustainable" wherever possible. I particularly loathe "sustainable living" which always brings images of zombies to my mind. Ultimately nothing sustains, and any attempt to attain that end will fail. If sustainability is treading water, resilience is swimming forward against the current. And actually, once you get the hang of it, the current shifts and flows with you.

Burning Down the House

"Protection, restoration and regeneration of ecosystems and communities are the keys to both mitigation and adaptation."

It is no secret we live in a house on fire.

This December in Paris world leaders will meet for the 21st time in 22 years in an ongoing attempt to form a bucket brigade and put out the fire. Each time the fire is larger and less easy to control, and each time they end up going home without throwing a single drop of water. Among the issues are where the buckets are, who will be at the front of the line and who at the back, whether those less responsible for starting the fire can opt out of the work, or even rekindle the fire if it starts to lag, and whether, on a cost-risk-benefit analysis, it might be better to let it burn for a few more years before taking time away from profitable economic activities.

At the outskirts of this debate will be those of us in the UN Observer community who are yelling at the muddled delegates standing around watching the fire to please, will you, just do something! Of course, among the screaming rabble will be those who are quite certain there is no problem and doing nothing is the right course, and those who have placed their fate and the world's in the hands of an all-knowing bearded Superman who can be relied on to save His chosen, even if everything else goes up in smoke. Their voices will blend with ours to make the cacophony even harder to parse.

We, the permaculture and ecovillage people, go to these crazy confabs because we have a simple solution to offer, a suite of tools that will counter the carbon menace and send it to ground, buying the human race time to deal with other game-enders - like the overfecundity of our species, Atoms for Peace, and Peak Everything, for instance.

As the International Permaculture Convergence in England was drawing to a close last month, we were in the big tent listening to Starhawk[51] read from the climate change working group's statement, a document intended to be taken to Paris to give voice to permaculture designers. There came an objection from a gentleman who clearly had not taken the time to educate himself on the subject of biochar and thus was of the opinion it was a Ponzi scheme or Snake Oil and wanted mention of it deleted. I held my tongue.

> Well you need not feel so all alone
> Everybody must get stoned
>
> - Bob Dylan, *Rainy Day Women* [52]

Having given extensive biochar talks at Permaculture Convergences in Jordan and Cuba, and more just recently in Iceland and England, including a controlled burn facilitated by Dale Hendricks[53] two days earlier, I thought I had already answered any skeptics in the permie crowd and won them over. This fellow was apparently a late arrival.

---

[51] Starhawk (born Miriam Simos on June 17, 1951) is an American writer and activist, author of *The Fifth Sacred Thing, The Spiral Dance,* and *The Earth Path.* She is known as a theorist of feminist neopaganism and ecofeminism.
[52] metrolyrics.com/rainy-day-women-lyrics-bob-dylan.html
[53] greenlightplants.com/

Starhawk had made biochar in a workshop in Belize the previous February, and I had gone over the ethical principles with her in Cuba and Jordan, so I knew she was no stranger to the questions. She deftly handled the heckler by making a small adjustment to the text, placing the words "sustainably produced" in front of the word "biochar" to acknowledge his point about the potential for misuse.

Having had a hand in the drafting of the document, I let it pass that this was the only use of the word "sustainable," a word I abhor, that crept in.

Still, the document is a good one, and so I'll reproduce it in its entirety:

International Permaculture Convergence, Gilwell Park, England, September 2015

Permaculture is a system of ecological design as well as a global movement of practitioners, educators, researchers and organizers, bound by three core ethics: care for the earth, care for the people and care for the future. Permaculture integrates knowledge and practices that draw from many disciplines and links them into solutions to meet human needs while ensuring a resilient future. With little funding or institutional support, this movement has spread over the past forty years and now represents projects on every inhabited continent.

The permaculture movement offers vital perspectives and tools to address catastrophic climate change.

Human-caused climate change is a crisis of systems - ecosystems and social systems - and must be addressed systemically. No single new technology or blanket solution will solve the problem. Permaculture employs systems thinking, looking at patterns, relationships and flows, linking solutions together into synergistic strategies that work with nature and fit local conditions, terrain, and cultures.

Efforts to address the climate crisis must be rooted in social, economic, and ecological justice. The barriers to solutions are political and social, not technical, and the impacts of climate change fall most heavily on frontline communities, who have done the least to cause it. Indigenous communities hold worldviews and perspectives that are vitally needed to help us come back into balance with the natural world. We must build and repair relationships across cultures and communities on a basis of respect, and the voices, leadership and needs of frontline and indigenous communities must be given prominence in all efforts to address the problem.

Permaculture ethics direct us to create abundance, share it fairly, and limit overconsumption in order to benefit the whole. Healthy, just, truly democratic communities are a potent antidote to climate change.

Both the use of fossil fuels and the mismanagement of land and resources are driving the climate crisis. We must shift from fire to flow: from burning oil, gas, coal and uranium to capturing flows of energy from sun, wind, and water in safe and renewable ways.

Soil is the key to sequestering excess carbon. By restoring the world's degraded soils, we can store carbon as soil fertility, heal degraded land, improve water cycles and quality, and produce healthy food and true abundance. Protection, restoration and regeneration of ecosystems and communities are the keys to both mitigation and adaptation.

Permaculture integrates knowledge, experience, research and practices from many disciplines to restore landscapes and communities on a large scale. These strategies include:

- A spectrum of safe, renewable energy technologies.

- Scientific research and exchange of knowledge, information and innovations.

- Water harvesting, retention and restoration of functional water systems.

- Forest conservation, reforestation and sustainable forestry.

- Regenerative agricultural practices - organic, no-till and low-till, polycultures, small-scale intensive systems and agroecology.

- Planned rotational grazing, grasslands restoration, and silvopasture systems.

- Agroforestry, food forests and perennial systems.

- Bioremediation and mycoremediation.

- Increasing soil organic carbon using biological methods: compost, compost teas, mulch, fungi, worms and beneficial microorganisms.

- Sustainably produced biochar for carbon capture and soil building.

- Protection and restoration of oceanic ecosystems.

- Community-based economic models, incorporating strategies such as co-operatives, local currencies, gift economies, and horizontal economic networks.

- Relocalization of food systems and economic enterprises to serve communities.

- Conservation, energy efficiency, re-use, recycling and full cost accounting.

- A shift to healthier, climate-friendly diets.

- Demonstration sites, model systems, ecovillages and intentional communities.

- Conflict transformation, trauma counseling and personal and spiritual healing.

- Transition Towns and other local movements to create community resilience.

- And many more!

None of these tools function alone. Each unique place on earth will require its own mosaic of techniques and practices to mitigate and adapt to climate change.

To deepen our knowledge of these approaches and refine our ability to apply and combine them, we need to fund and support unbiased, independent scientific research.

Each one of us has a unique and vital role to play in meeting this greatest of global challenges. The crisis is grave, but if together we meet it with hope and action, we have the tools we need to create a world that is healthy, balanced, vibrant, just, abundant and beautiful.

The Next Tango in Paris

"Sweden has decided to decommission all its nuclear plants but has yet to propose a similar program to phase out its wind turbines."

"Carbon-neutral is so 20th century. We really need to get beyond zero. That is what ecovillages can offer."

I was just concluding a conference call for Global Ecovillage Network delegates in the run-up to the UN climate summit one month from now in Paris when I said that. The discussion had turned to what our message should be. There is a very good program initiated by ten European ecovillages, called the Fossil-Fuel Free Community Challenge. It is very ambitious, and tracks what Sweden, already carbon-neutral, has recently pledged.

It is one thing to gradually wean yourself from fossil energy by increments, such as by putting a tax on carbon at the source, as Al Gore tried unsuccessfully to do in 1992, or to strip the fossil industry of its obscene subsidies, as Bill McKibben[54] urges. It is quite another to go cold turkey.

Costa Rica met its entire national power demand using renewable energy for 75 consecutive days this year, but that was only electricity, and anyway, it was Costa Rica. On a spectacularly windy day this past July, Denmark generated 140% of its electrical power from wind alone.

---

[54] Bill McKibben is an American environmentalist, author, and journalist who has written extensively on the impact of climate change. He is the Schumann Distinguished Scholar at Middlebury College and advisor to the climate campaign group 350.org.

A recent study by Mark Jacobson, David Blittersdorf, and Tom Murphy, originally published by The Energy XChange on September 1, 2015[55], shows its quite possible to switch the whole world to renewables right now, at no net cost, albeit not quite at the same profligacy standard.

To get off carbon, Sweden will have to close its nuclear plants, which have a carbon footprint of about 16 kg CO2e per MWh[56] despite what technophiles James Hansen, George Monbiot, Ken Caldiera, or James Lovelock, having drunk the Atomic Kool Aid, may tell you about nuclear power being carbon-free. Wind power, by contrast, generates 10 kg per MWh. Some countries may join Sweden in deciding to decommission all their nuclear plants, but none has yet to propose a similar program to phase out wind turbines.

Personally we have no problem endorsing a massive switch to renewables and the sooner the better, but one also needs to place a caveat under that about it not exactly replacing fossil fuels. Nor will it salvage consumer culture.

If one were to think of it in terms of megajoules[57] of energy, we were living off a current account of sunlight up until about 200 years ago, when we discovered that earth had been frugally putting aside a billion-year pension account all this time. That was supposed to help the planet go nova when the Sun runs out of hydrogen. What did we do? We started withdrawing, gradually at first, then faster, and now as fast as we possibly can. We have withdrawn a little more than half of that inheritance now, mainly the

---

[55] energyx.org/will-renewables-replace-fossil-fuels/
[56] kilograms CO2 per megawatt-hour of electricity generated
[57] The work required to produce one watt of power for one second, or one "watt second" (W·s) (compare kilowatt hour - 3.6 megajoules).

easy-to-reach part. We can't withdraw the remainder because (a) it costs more than we can afford to spend; and (b) it would fry the planet. So we are slowly coming to the realization that we may have to return to our former mainstay, the current income account; you know, the sunlight.

The savings account was a very rich endowment, though. Eating through 500 million years of fossil sunlight in 200 years enabled each of us to have hundreds of energy slaves at our beck and call. As Richard Heinberg says, a cup of gasoline can take a 2-ton truck over a mountain. How many horses would have to be fed how much grain to accomplish the same task? How many hours of wind generators charging batteries? Heinberg points out:

> Making pig iron - the main ingredient in steel - requires blast furnaces. Making cement requires 100-meter-long kilns that operate at 1500 degrees C. In principle it is possible to produce high heat for these purposes with electricity or giant solar collectors, but nobody does it that way now because it would be much more expensive than burning coal or natural gas. Crucially, current manufacturing processes for building solar panels and wind turbines also depend upon high-temperature industrial processes fueled by oil, coal, and natural gas. Again, alternative ways of producing this heat are feasible in principle - but the result would probably be significantly higher-cost solar and wind power. And there are no demonstration projects to show us just how easy or hard this would be.

Zero carbon power, or zero fossil fuels, while a wonderful goal, and one put out by Greenpeace USA and 350.org, will entail more sacrifice than many people, including even the Swedes, understand. For one thing, the energy return on energy invested (EROEI) is less than 4:1 for wind, which is marginal and produces only electricity, unless you are pumping water. Biofuels are 1:1.4, or negative return. Corn ethanol costs more BTU - and horsepower - to make than it can provide when combusted. Contrast fossil fuels at historical returns of 100:1 to 40:1 (although falling off the precipice now as we spend more to obtain less).

Electrification of all sectors - heating, cooling, industrial processes, and transportation - would be implicit to an all-renewable economy. But we would need to reduce total energy use by approximately 70 percent, maybe more, to make that switch. Efficiency improvements could potentially take us part way but not all the way.

If there is one thing ecovillages should be good at, it is making crisis mitigation fun. We weary of the hair shirt approach to mitigating climate change. We can cut consumption and party, too. But then Europe, particularly the Scandinavian countries, have a "set an impossible goal and lead by example" culture when it comes to climate negotiations. Not only have they not gotten any other countries to go along, but also their own populations have balked at the austerity required, throwing out progressive governments and replacing them with conservatives, who are anything but conservers, Ponzi'ing up bigger mountains of debt and fattening the larders of banksters with the proceeds of liquidated public assets.

Sure, we have some great fossil-fuel free islands in Denmark and a bicycle autobahn in Germany, but honestly, how many businessmen do you know who would garage the BMW in favor of a 15-speed Hase Spezialräder for that meeting in Bonn, especially in winter?

The alternative we have proposed is to net-sequester - go beyond zero - at the home, village, and regional scale. The tools we have for accomplishing this are many - carbon farming, eco-agroforestry, biomass energy with carbon capture, and biochar in everything from clothing to buildings.

These simple changes can switch civilization from its current trajectory - one that ensures near-term human extinction (NTHE) - to something I have been calling Civilization 2.0, which returns the planet to something approximating the comfortable Holocene in which we evolved, within a reasonable time. The time variable is the unknown here, because it is unlikely that COP21, with its low ambition, will do much to speed the necessary conversion.

Will it be possible to live in the high style of consumer culture in Civilization 2.0? No chance. But we can continue living, and have quite abundant, happy lives, and that is no small deal. The alternative really is NTHE.

George Monbiot writes:

> Governments ignore issues when the media ignores them. And the media ignores them because ... well there's a question with a thousand answers, many of which involve power. But one reason is the complete failure of perspective in a deskilled industry dominated by corporate press releases, photo ops and fashion shoots, where everyone seems to be waiting for everyone else to take a lead. The media makes a collective non-decision to treat this catastrophe as a non-issue, and we all carry on as if it's not happening.

At the climate summit in Paris in December, the media, trapped within the intergovernmental bubble of abstract diplomacy and manufactured drama, will cover the negotiations almost without reference to what is happening elsewhere. The talks will be removed to a realm with which we have no moral contact. And, when the circus moves on, the silence will resume. Is there any other industry that serves its customers so badly?

Our my first night in town, after picking up my credentials at Le Bourget and checking in at The Place 2B, I took the metro with photographer Carolyn Monsastra to a rehabilitated factory that had, more than a century earlier, been one of Paris's prides - the *"C'ie Parisienne de Distribution d' Electricite"* in *Le Generale.* Now the parapet's decorative cornice lunette clerestories were boarded with plywood to hide broken glass, the riveted exposed-steel I-beams that had been kept painted white were chipping and rusting, and the entrance of the building was through an imposing, steel barred metal door off the sidewalk that bore a simple, handwritten, butcher-paper-and-masking-tape sign saying, "Transition COP 21 ~ Bienvenue." Inside, Christmas lights were being strung to put a festive air on the old place and a large projection screen was hung for the evening's speakers to show their slides.

The featured guest was English writer and activist Rob Hopkins, whose 12-step method for weaning any community from fossil fuel and climate vulnerability had spread like the plague through the social activist centers of Europe. Its success was a product of its irrepressible optimism and from designing, in real terms in real places, a new kind of wealth built upon social and natural capital. Rob was there to attend the COP the next week and he brought along his latest book, *21 Stories of Transition: How a Movement of Communities is Coming Together to Reimagine and Rebuild the World.*

I did not record the inspiring talk he gave, but Rob was kind enough to recap it a few days later in his blog post for Transition Culture:

> Change happens in interesting ways. For example, recently, a community campaign where I live challenged a large local charitable organization's land use decisions, in particular its decision to submit large swaths of land for development. The community campaign questioned the link between the organization's stated values and its actions. Looking back in hindsight, it's interesting to see how the change unfolded, and how there is no one single Great Change Moment to point to. But at the moment when the then CEO of the organization was brazening it out, telling everyone how the organization was listening and responding when it was clear that it really wasn't, the ground had been eaten away from under him, and his were empty words, and a month later he stood down. Events were moving, the world around him was changing; he had been left behind.
>
> Similarly the GDR, East Germany, looked to be robust, powerful and permanent in the days before the Berlin Wall came down. In reality, we now know, it was holed below the waterline, undermined by the number of young people defecting to the West, corruption, rigged elections and much more. But until the Wall came down, you'd never have known. So how can we know, in the moment, which point in time we might point to as the moment when the change actually happened?
>
> While Paris looks likely to not be that Great Change Moment, perhaps it is we who need to take a different

approach here. Our role in Paris, or during that time, in my opinion, is not to see this event as a Great Change Moment, rather as just yet another important step in the ongoing - and of course massively urgent - building of a new, low carbon world. Instead, we should focus, during that time, on celebrating what is already happening. And there is much to celebrate.

Like Rob, the transition team, or the permaculture folk, I travel to these fetes and hang out my wares so that passersby can notice and lodge this new meme somewhere in the back of their brains. When things get bad enough, perhaps the meme can move from niche to mainstream. It is already all ready.

Saturday, November 28, 2015

On the Ground in Le Bourget

What if there were a bottom-up alternative that was not theoretical but has been already successfully demonstrated for the past 20 years, with millions of people participating?

When I booked my flight to Paris in the summer, there had been only 2 seats left on the flight I wanted, even though it was a jumbo Air France jet. When we boarded in Detroit at 8 pm, however, the plane was two-thirds empty and I could pick any vacant four seats I wanted to take my blanket and pillow to after supper.

The reason the plane was empty was that most people are cowards. There is less risk of being out and about in Paris, than in, say, San Bernardino, California, and yet the terror attack hitting a Paris stadium concert and outdoor cafe the weekend before made everyone nervous and airlines suffered mass cancellations. Alec Baldwin told Max Keiser that many celebrities had planned to come for the COP, but decided otherwise out of safety concerns.

DeGaulle airport had surprisingly light security on Saturday morning. I arrived at sunrise, in light rain and mild cold, proceeded through customs, and exited without inspection. I could not locate the Navigo kiosk where I had been advised by GEN's Paris coordinator, Marti Mueller, to pick up a week-length 5-zone pass, so I just paid 10 euros for a trip to Le Bourget.

The system the UN security division had set up was to isolate all arrivals to a single rail stop and then use hybrid electric shuttle buses for the 15-to-30 minute ride (depending on traffic) to the convention center complex at the old airfield where Charles Lindbergh had landed the Spirit of St. Louis at the start of the Aviation Age. The shuttles passed easily through military cordons and deposited us at the plywood ramps leading through painted wooden columns to the glass portico of the entrance building. There security suddenly stepped up.

First we passed through a watchful gaggle of state police and military, some with sniffer dogs, to a suited UN security team asking to see ID. I showed my invitation and passport and was waved ahead to the next stop, which was to pre-screen my roller bag before being allowed into the queue. I opened the bag and displayed a week's worth of clean clothing, then was told to zip up and move on. Then came the scanners, which were magnetic - the rule in Europe - not invasive and cancerous, as they are in the US. I removed belt, watch, laptop, phone, everything in my pockets, but not my shoes, and walked through. No query about the Biolite or Beaner stoves; they went through the X-rays and did not raise any concerns.

Getting my credentials was easier than I thought. They already had my photo on file, so once I passed the bar code on my invitation letter under their scanner, it was no more than ten seconds before I was handed a blue lanyard and my freshly minted plastic UN name badge. Mission accomplished, I wheeled around and headed for the shuttle back to the rail station.

This time the fare was just 2 euros, and before long I found myself at Gare du Nord and walking up Rue de Dunkerque to The Place 2B, an activist hub with a 300-bed hostel, the St. Christopher's Inn, attached. This would be my center of coordination and culture for the next two weeks.

I am part of a Global Ecovillage Network diplomatic team. Owing to my availability back in April to steer the effort to register 14 of us with the COP-21 secretariat and get a maximum of four of us badged and a side-event scheduled, I am now Head of Delegation, although I do not intuit that to give me any special power or even the ability to chair meetings. It merely means that when we need to interface with the UN over any issues of credentials, access, or space, I have to swing into action personally.

I think one of the advantages that I gained from competitive sports, theater, debate, and similar experiences in childhood is that competition prepares you mentally for coping with your own fears and insecurity. In a twenty-year career as an appellate attorney, including arguments at the US Supreme Court on multiple occasions, I learned to cope with the fear of failure - and with the physical manifestations of stage fright; butterflies, nausea, cold sweat - by thorough preparation and a good night's sleep. The fear of public speaking is one that most normal people have, and it is healthy. It must be overcome from time to time if we are to benefit from shared wisdom. For me, preparation gives confidence, and after that, I cultivate a Buddhist sense of non-attachment to the outcome.

Our side event will be at 4:45 pm on the first Saturday of the COP, inside the Blue Zone, where one needs a special badge to access the room. Our subject is Ecovillages: 1001 Solutions to Climate Change, and I have been preparing my 15-minute part of it for most of the year, with prepared and improvised talks before trial audiences in Belize, Iceland, England, New Mexico and Tennessee before coming to Paris. The UN coordinating office has asked for a short description that will go out in the daily program, and GEN also wants to print a flyer to pass out in our booth and leave around various parts of the COP, so I have been busy crafting the text. Here is what I came up with:

You are invited to a presentation by the Global Ecovillage Network (GEN), Green Korea, and Asociación Proteger:

ECOVILLAGES; 1001 SOLUTIONS TO CLIMATE CHANGE

When: Saturday 05 Dec 2015 16:45-18:15
Where: Le Bourget Observer rm 01

The delay in addressing climate change now compels us to go beyond zero in actively removing more greenhouse gases than we emit, billions of tons per year, starting at once. Many theories exist on how to accomplish this, but most involve expensive or untested technology imposed from the top down through taxes, regulations, or complex finance. What if there was a bottom- up alternative that was not theoretical but has been already successfully demonstrated for the past 20 years, with millions of people participating? What if this model could scale rapidly on its own momentum, in all cultures and locations? Many of todays ecovillages are so successful they are able to proactively assist with disaster relief, refugee resettlement, and poverty alleviation. Amid a perfect storm of bad news, here is a ray of light.

16:45-17:00: Sarah Queblatin, Networking and Outreach Coordinator, Global Ecovillage Network (moderator), Introduction
17:00-17:15: Ms. Geun Jeong Shin, Green Korea: Grass Roots Alternatives to the Fukushima energy path for Korea
17:15-17:30: Liliana Lewinski and Richard Siren, Asociación Proteger: Indigenous rights and community life in the rural and vulnerable context; low carbon vernacular and the role of aesthetics.
17:30-17:45: Kosha Anja Joubert, GEN CEO: (by skype) Ecovillage: 1001 Solutions to Climate Change.
17:45-18:00: Albert Bates, GEN and eCO2; Going Beyond Zero, Case Studies
18:00-18:15: Open Discussion

Please join us for a look at a hopeful future! Registration not required; seating first-come, first-serve.

Our booth, in the Green Zone, the "Climate Generations" area, is provided by ECOLISE, a coalition of European non-profits founded in part by GEN-Europe. Robert Hall, native of California and citizen of Sweden, is currently the President of Global Ecovillage Network of Europe and sits on the GEN international board. He reminds me a bit of Richard Gere or John Denver, thick, thatched greying hair over fine eyes and a Colorado-rugged face. He arrived in Paris from Suderbyn Permaculture Ecovillage located on Gotland - an island in the Baltic Sea, along with another Suderbynese villager, Alisa Sidorenko, a pretty blond-over-brunette with skin-tight lycra slacks tucked into fleece-lined boots, very Swedish, but whose accent betrays she is originally Russian, raised in Khazakstan.

Like most of our delegation, Robert and Alisa have all the skills and credentials they'd need to speak with diplomats. She finished her first master's degree in technical engineering studies in Russia, her second in Sustainable Development in Sweden. He is a graduate in International Relations from University of California, Davis; has a second degree in Economics from Lund, and a Master of Science in Environmental Engineering and Sustainable Infrastructure from the Royal Institute of Technology, Stockholm. He has lived, studied and worked in more than 10 countries on 4 continents, including prior gigs in sustainable development and democratic governance for the United Nations (UNDP and FAO), European Commission, Organization for Security and Cooperation in Europe, and the Swedish International Development Cooperation Agency.

I need not go into all the talent brought to our Climate Generations exhibit, but ECOLISE was able to purchase the space with the help of GEN, Permaculture Climate Group, Transition Towns Network, Sail Transport Network, and others. GEN's team includes its President, Kosha Joubert, Gaia Trust's Ross Jackson, Gaia Education's May East, GEN's permanent UN representative Rob Wheeler, GEN International Networking and Outreach Coordinator Sarah Queblatin, and many more. Dr. Marian Zeitlin, Emerita Professor of Tufts whose career in nutritional biochemistry and international nutrition planning (USAID, UNESCO, World Bank) goes back to 1977, founded the first African national network of the Global Ecovillage Network in 2002, GEN-Senegal. Tim Clarke, who has an Oxford master's in Food Resources and Community Development, is now with the International Institute for Environment and Development and a board member of the Jane Goodall Institute. He was formerly the Head of Division, Crisis Management and Planning Directorate of the EU's European External Action Service, EU Ambassador to Tanzania and the East African Community (with an operation budget of over €1 billion) and served in the trenches as an EU government honcho for many development projects over many years.

We were not starved for talent. We brought a boatload of it. Ironically, this makes preparation of our speaking event all the more challenging. We have to squeeze all of this collective wisdom into a tiny slot, accessible by only two of us, and shared with two NGOs we have never worked with before.

Paris: Le Overture

"The 'guard rail' concept, which implies a warming limit that guarantees full protection from dangerous anthropogenic interference, no longer works. What is called for is a consideration of societally acceptable risk."

Today I am finally in Paris, site of COP-21. I have been reporting from these conferences for my blog since early 2008, with the run-up to COP-15 in Copenhagen. Each time there has been much ado about the potential for transformative action and each time, by the end of the two weeks, it turns into just *adieu* and see you next year.

The past three conferences in particular (Doha 2012, Warsaw 2013, Lima 2014) were really just treading water, trying to iron out differences enough to proceed to a formal, legally binding document to be adopted here in Paris this year, in 14 days' time.

In 1992 at the Rio Earth Summit, the UN member countries negotiated an international treaty to cooperatively consider what they could do to limit average global temperature increases and to cope with whatever other impacts of reckless fossil fuel use were, by then, inevitable. These annual conferences at the beginning of every December were intended to reach those decisions.

It took only three years for the COPs to recognize that the minor emission reductions they had imagined at first glance in the giddy Summit at Rio would be totally inadequate. So, they launched negotiations to strengthen the international response and, two years later, in 1997, adopted the Kyoto Protocol. The Protocol legally bound overdeveloped countries to emission reduction targets while giving the underdeveloping countries a pass. This eventually caused a lot of friction, because many of the countries who got passes, China and India for instance, took that opportunity to build hundreds of coal-fired power plants and become the world's leading greenhouse gas polluters.

The US Head Negotiator, Todd Stern, told the *Guardian:*

> We have a situation where 60-65% of emissions come from developing countries. That's a good thing. It means that developing countries are developing. But you cannot solve climate change on the back of the 35%.

A watershed moment for the negotiating process occurred in Copenhagen when the world was on the verge of enacting a binding treaty to replace Kyoto, with everyone included and sanctions for scofflaws. At the last moment Hillary Clinton and Barack Obama swooped in and snatched defeat from the jaws of victory, substituting a voluntary pledge system (Independent Nationally Determined Contributions, all non-binding) that only 5 countries were willing to sign, but it was enough to torpedo the treaty. In a recent Presidential campaign debate, Ms. Clinton called it one of her great moments of leadership on the climate issue, which rescued the Copenhagen talks.

President Obama, for his part, recalled it this way:

> And Copenhagen, although it was a disorganized mess - and I still remember flying in that last day, and nothing was happening, and I literally had to rescue the entire enterprise by crashing a meeting of the BRIC countries [Brazil, Russia, India and China] and strong-arming them into coming up with at least a document that could build some consensus going into the future.

What we were able to do was to establish the basic principle that it wasn't going to be enough just for the advanced countries to act - that China, India, others, despite having much lower per-capita carbon footprints, given the sheer size of their populations and how rapidly they were developing, were going to have to put some skin in the game as well.

It is true there were differences of opinion about how close Copenhagen was to actually sealing the deal. "By the time [Obama arrived in Copenhagen] things had already unraveled and then had to be put back together," according to Ben Rhodes, deputy national security adviser for strategic communications at the White House. Rhodes said that in Paris Obama's tactics would be different. "The goal here is to give a push with heads of state at the beginning of the process and then allow [Secretary of State John] Kerry and others to finalize the details."

The Kyoto's protocol's first commitment period started in 2008 and ended in 2012. Despite the debacle in Copenhagen, most of the European countries hit their targets. Total emissions for all other overdeveloped countries rose by about 10 percent. China's rose about 10 percent per year, and it is now the world's largest emitter. Canada was committed to cutting its greenhouse emissions to 6% below 1990 levels by 2012, but in 2009 emissions were 17% higher than in 1990 and the Harper government prioritized tar sand development in Alberta. Canada's emissions are now up 34% from baseline and Australia is in similar territory. In Doha at COP-18, 36 UN member states agreed to extend Kyoto for another round, beginning in 2013 and running to 2020, but without the major polluters on board it is a feeble effort.

Kyoto is generally viewed as a limited success. Among the overdeveloped, France, the UK, and Germany achieved reductions of 7, 15 and 19 percent. In any event, these reductions pale when compared to the impact of peat fires in Indonesia, deforestation in Brazil, or methane releases in Siberia.

At COP-16 in 2010, the rest of the world, recognizing that the United States had been allowed to hijack the Copenhagen meeting, put the UN multiparty process back on track with the Cancun Agreements. Fast start finance (a.k.a. dollar diplomacy) brought pledges from the US and Europe to mobilize through international institutions, approaching 30 billion US dollars for the period 2010-2012. Funding for adaptation was allocated to the most vulnerable underdeveloping countries, such as small island states and equatorial Africa, but nobody really knows whether or when that money will show up.

At Paris the various governments are "invited" to provide information on their efforts to reduce emissions (calculated, for the underdeveloping, as reductions on theoretical maximum development burn - Business As Usual, or BAU - to more modest, "responsible," but nonetheless increased burns) and to please let everyone know how soon and by what means the promised great wealth transfer will take place.

Nonetheless, by slow increments, the noose is gradually tightening around the neck of fossil fuel companies and their government backers. All governments recommitted in Durban to a comprehensive plan that would come closer over time to delivering the ultimate objective of the Convention: to stabilize greenhouse gas concentrations in the atmosphere at a level that would "prevent dangerous human interference with the climate system" and at the same time preserve the rights of the 5 billion world poor to "sustainable development." Let us set aside for a moment the incompatibility of those two goals as their terms are presently defined.

Durban made two very important adjustments to the Cancun Agreements. First, that COP said that science would trump politics and that if it should be proven, for instance, that 2 degrees is not a sufficient guardrail to prevent human civilization from veering over the cliff into dangerous climate change, the goal can adjust. A scientific review process was established to monitor the goal and "to ensure that collective action is adequate to prevent the average global temperature rising beyond the agreed limit."

Secondly, the Durban COP said very firmly that the 2015 COP in Paris would deliver "a new and universal greenhouse gas reduction protocol, legal instrument or other outcome with legal force that would set requirements for the period beyond 2020." This specification of a "legal instrument" or "legal force" was agreed to by the United States, China, and the other key players right there in Durban with the whole world watching.

The likelihood Paris will produce a binding treaty was cast into doubt when the *Financial Times* interviewed US Secretary of State John Kerry a few weeks ago. Kerry told *FT* there were "not going to be legally binding reduction targets like Kyoto."

French President Hollande immediately replied in the press that "if the agreement is not legally binding, there will be no agreement. We must give the Paris agreement, if there is one, a binding character in the sense that the commitments that are made must be kept and respected."

"This is not hot air. This is a real agreement, with real terms," said French Foreign Minister Laurent Fabius.

Backpedaling under fire, a spokesperson for the US State Department told *The New York Times* that while the *FT* article "may have been read to suggest that the US supports a completely nonbinding approach ... that is not the case, and is not Secretary Kerry's position."

COP-18 in Doha was, as we said, the start of the Paris prelude. One significant bump was release of The World Bank's "Turn Down the Heat: Why a 4°C Warmer World Must Be Avoided," showing that the world is on track towards a 4 degrees Celsius temperature rise, should the currently inadequate level of ambition remain. Doha responded to that challenge by triggering the Durban process to review the long-term temperature goal. They set up a Structured Expert Dialog - 70 wise men - that was to start in 2013 and conclude by 2015.

COP-19 in Warsaw moved us a little closer. The rulebook for reducing emissions from deforestation and forest degradation (REDD) was agreed, together with measures to bolster forest preservation and a results-based payment system to promote forest protection. Overdeveloped countries met the target capitalization of $100 million for the Adaptation Fund, which can now fund priority projects. Governments established the Warsaw International Mechanism for Loss and Damage to address losses and damages associated with long-term climate change impacts in countries that are especially vulnerable to such impacts.

COP-20 in Lima was more of the same, more agenda-setting for the run-up to Paris and the signing of a formal treaty. It came close to faltering over the issue of "common but differentiated responsibilities" (the distinction between the expected pledges from overdeveloped and underdeveloping Parties). At COP-17 in Durban in 2011, countries agreed that the post-2020 actions to be negotiated in Paris would be "applicable to all." Alton Meyer of the Union of Concerned Scientists observed:

> The differentiation issue nearly blocked the final decision in Lima, where the stakes were actually quite small. In Paris next year, the stakes will be quite high: nothing less than the shape of the climate regime for the next several decades. It will not be possible to paper over sharp differences on this issue with artful language that different groupings can interpret in a way favorable to their position, as happened in the last hours of Lima.

The anticipated report of the meeting of the 70 wise men, the Structured Expert Dialog or SED, was issued in February 2015 and reviewed by government delegates at the pre-COP meeting in Bonn in June. This is a very important 180-page document and worth spending some time to read.

The document divides the dialog into three parts:

> Theme 1 - the adequacy of the long-term global goal in the light of the ultimate objective;
>
> Theme 2 - overall progress made towards achieving the long-term global goal;
>
> Theme 3 - consideration of strengthening the long-term global goal.

It starts off addressing whether temperature is an adequate warning gauge for climate change:

> Message 1: A long-term global goal defined by a temperature limit serves its purpose well…. Adding other limits to the long-term global goal, such as sea level rise or ocean acidification, only reinforces the basic finding emerging from the analysis of the temperature limit, namely that we need to take urgent and strong action to reduce GHG emissions.

That is followed by this rather disturbing chart, previously published in the latest assessment of the Intergovernmental Panel on Climate Change (IPCC):

The relationship between global average temperature change, risks from climate change, cumulative anthropogenic carbon dioxide emissions and changes in global annual greenhouse gas emissions by 2050 relative to 2010 for 2 °C of warming above pre-industrial levels

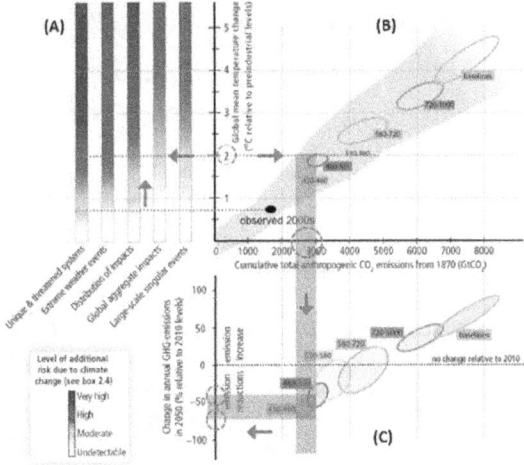

Source: Adapted from the summary for policymakers in the Synthesis Report of the Fifth Assessment Report of the Intergovernmental Panel on Climate Change, figure SPM.10.
Note: Limiting aggregated risks from climate change (panel A) by a global average temperature limit of 2 °C (blue/red circle in panel B) implies, through the limited carbon budget (red circle at bottom of panel B), a reduction in annual GHG emissions of 40–70 per cent relative to 2010 emissions by 2050 (red circles in panel C).
Abbreviation: GHG = greenhouse gas.

On the Y (vertical) axis is temperature change in degrees C. To the left of the vertical axis line is a set of brightly colored bar graphs (grey-to-black in this book) representing corresponding risks of each degree of warming.

Things to note:

Two degrees is far from safe. It represents "dangerous interference with climate systems," to quote the Framework Convention.

At 1.5 degrees there is a high degree of likelihood we will lose unique and threatened systems and experience extreme weather events. (Note, the risk of extreme weather at today's 1-degree elevation is considered moderate). At 2 degrees these move into darker shades and the distribution of impacts becomes high, meaning almost no one escapes.

On the (horizontal) X-axis are the cumulative total emissions of CO_2 since 1870. Right now we have taken about 2500 $GtCO_2$ out of the ground, resulting in a net atmospheric concentration of 400 ppm. The chart reports that we could probably go to 4000 $GtCO_2$ and 580 ppm before we exceed the 2-degree limit. This is dangerous nonsense and one is left scratching one's head at how this could have been decided. It guarantees resumption of that food fight between India, Indonesia, South Africa, Brazil, and others about how many "parking spaces" in that big parking lot in the sky remain for "sustainable development" (read: still-to-be-constructed coal plants).

Here is a short run-down of the other messages of the Structured Expert Dialog:

On Theme 1:

Limiting global warming to below 2 °C necessitates a radical transition (deep decarbonization now and going forward), not merely a fine-tuning of current trends.

Risks will be increasingly unevenly distributed; responses need to be made by each location.

The "guard rail" concept, which implies a warming limit that guarantees full protection from dangerous anthropogenic interference, no longer works. What is called for is a consideration of societally acceptable risk.

At 4 degrees effects are non-linear, more than double 2 degrees. The catch potential of fisheries would be greatly reduced, and crop production would be beyond adaptation in many areas. Sea level rise would far exceed 1 m.

On Theme 2:

We know how to measure progress on mitigation but not on adaptation.

The world is not on track to achieve the long-term global goal, but successful mitigation policies are known and must be scaled up urgently.

Under present economic regimes, spending on "brown" technologies will continue to grow faster than spending on green technologies.

Scaling up means putting a price on carbon and promoting low-carbon technologies, so that their share becomes dominant.

On Theme 3:

The "guardrail" concept, in which up to 2°C of warming is considered safe, is inadequate and would therefore be better seen as an upper limit, a defense line that needs to be stringently defended, while less warming would be preferable.

Limiting global warming to below 2°C is still feasible and will bring about many co-benefits, but poses substantial technological, economic and institutional challenges.

Parties may wish to take a precautionary route by aiming for limiting global warming as far below 2°C as possible, discarding the notion of a guardrail but thinking more of a defense line or even a buffer zone.

These important points were harvested from the Dialog and processed into recommendations to be given to the COP, at not inconsiderable time and expense. Sadly, as we shall see, the official delegations and heads of state would never receive the substantive recommendations, because they will be blocked by Saudi Arabia with the assistance of India and China.

Paris First Movement

"The Paris talks are doomed even if they succeed, because even if they succeed they will have won the wrong argument."

On November 17 we heard David Wasdell, of Project Gaia-Apollo and Team Leader of the Global System Dynamics and Policy Co-ordination Action of the European Commission, speaking on Radio Ecoshock. His overriding theme: 2 degrees is not safe; we are past the point of safe now; and we need to get back to safe as rapidly as we can. The timetables given by the Structured Expert Dialogue (SED), or what I called the "70 wise men" in my previous chapter, would, according to Wasdell, be disastrous if implemented.

His arguments were very cogent, and based on solid evidence, but I had to ask myself why this person, who is not a climate scientist (he is a self-described "systems analyst") should hold greater credibility than 70 of the world's best climatologists? I am someone who has never given the Wizard of Oz a blank check but peers behind the curtain. As I picked through both sides - Wasdell's several PDF and video presentations and the SED report to the UNFCCC - I found undeniable logic in his and indefensible logic in theirs. Here is a segment from Wasdell's radio interview:

> David Wasdell: The set of computer models used by the IPCC only work with the feedback mechanisms that can be quantified. Inevitably that only gives part of the picture. In contrast, the history of planetary change includes by definition all the feedback processes, known and unknown, positive and negative (that is amplifying or damping),

together with all the complex interactions between them. The computer models predict that the temperature change from doubling the concentration of CO_2 would be about 3°C. Using the history of the actual relationship between temperature and CO_2 concentration we find the outcome is more like 8°C. That is a huge difference with massive strategic implications. The reality of Earth System Sensitivity is about 2 and a half times that stemming from the partial computer models.

***

Moving from the specific example of change since the last ice-age, we can derive the value of the more generalized "Climate Sensitivity," the equilibrium change in average surface temperature of the planet following a doubling of the concentration of atmospheric CO_2. The temperature change required to compensate for the effect of doubling concentration of CO_2 on its own is calculated to be 0.97°C. Climate sensitivity when only fast feedbacks are taken into consideration stands at 3°C. Including the effects of the carbon-cycle feedbacks raises the value of Climate Sensitivity to 4.5°C. Adding the contribution from the ice-sheet dynamics correlates with a 6°C value for Climate Sensitivity, while the Sensitivity value representing the equilibrium dynamics of the Earth System as a whole stands at 7.8°C. Though please note that this figure is derived from slow and close to equilibrium conditions of change in the Quaternary period. It may be too low in the current conditions of the Anthropocene.

Now if you are working with computer models using only the fast feedbacks, you would predict that 2°C would be achieved at around 440 ppm. But if you are using Earth System Sensitivity, then at 440 ppm [which we will likely hit between 2030 and 2035] we would be looking at more like 5°C of change. However, as I keep reminding you, the computer simulation, inadequate and partial though it may be, is what is still being fed into the process of strategic policy-making on the assumption that the temperature change will only be 2°C for a concentration of 440 ppm of CO_2.

***

Alex Smith: At various conferences, in the business press and in scientific circles, there has been a lot of effort to work out how much carbon we can still burn, in the form of oil, gas, and coal, and still remain below the supposed 2-degree warming safety limit. No doubt diplomats at the Paris Conference will talk about this "carbon budget." How much of a budget do we really have left?

David Wasdell: At present the CO_2 concentration stands at 400 ppm. If it is thought to be safe to go up to 440 ppm, then we have a good budget to play with. There is still plenty of room in the sky-fill site. However, if we don't use the inadequate computer models, and instead apply the real Earth System Sensitivity, then we were already committed to passing the 2°C ceiling when CO_2 concentration stood at 334 ppm. That was back in 1978. We have already overspent the budget by a large amount! Getting the picture?

***

National promises [so-called 'INDCs' or Independent Nationally Determined Contributions] concerning reduction in CO_2 emissions have been [brought to the table] ahead of the COP-21 in Paris. Those promises look like pushing us to about 700 ppm by the end of the century (if they are implemented, and there is no guarantee about that whatsoever!). Business as usual is driving us up towards 800 or 900 ppm up here. If we cannot improve the level of promised emissions reduction, then "We might hit 4°C," predicts the IPCC using its low value for sensitivity. But if we use the full Earth System Sensitivity to examine the way the climate behaves at the level of 700 ppm, we are not looking at something around 4°C, but an increase of more like 10°C. That is twice the temperature shift between the ice ages and the pre-industrial benchmark. If we are not able to cut back on our current "business as usual" behavior, then the temperature rise increases to more like 12 or even 15°C (and two or three times that amount in the Arctic)! Goodbye all the ice on earth. Welcome to something like 90 feet of sea level rise, or even more when all the Greenland ice cap and the whole of the Antarctic ice sheet melts. Civilization would have collapsed and we would have evacuated London and New York well before then!

As delegates and heads of state from more than 195 countries gather here in Paris, the premises of the negotiations are badly flawed. It is as though the world's best negotiators are about to try to land a heavy passenger aircraft but the altimeter gauge is off by 500 feet. Despite being summoned in a timely fashion, the technicians who were brought in to repair the instrument either failed to do so, or have not been listened to, and thus we glide now towards a predictably unfavorable outcome. The Paris talks are doomed even if they succeed, because even if they succeed they will have won the wrong argument.

The Subsidiary Body for Scientific and Technological Advice (SBSTA) and the Subsidiary Body for Implementation (SBI) will continue to jointly consider the report of the Structured Expert Dialogue (SED) on the 2013-2015 review at the upcoming session to be held in Paris in December 2015, with a view to concluding their considerations on this matter and reporting their findings to the COP, which shall take appropriate action based on the review.

- UNFCCC

At Bonn in June, when the SED report was released, the negotiators asked hard questions of the Science Group, seeking these clarifications:

- the window of opportunity for staying under 2°C of warming and the risks created by overshooting,

- the practicality of achieving negative emissions,

- the marginal costs of mitigation for 40-70 percent emission reduction from 2010 levels by 2050,

- the Cancun pledges (INDCs),

- the impact of mitigation on economic growth, and

- production-versus-consumption-based accounting for emissions.

The answers coming back from the SED group were poorly informed and unimaginative. So, for instance, in response to the window of available time they said it would depend on how fast low-carbon technologies could scale, and that would be known by 2030 [at 430 ppm], but not much before then. As to the practicality of achieving negative emissions, the scientists seemed to be oblivious to the applications of biochar and the potential for cool energy, cool food, and cool building. They lamely opined that: "The practicability of negative emissions depends on costs, trade-offs, and the feasibility of various scenarios. The IPCC presented options for generating large amounts of energy from BECS [Biomass Energy with Carbon Capture and Storage] and the associated risks for biodiversity and food security and prices, stressing that policymakers need to consider the

119

trade-offs" [translation: consider unregulated use of genetically engineered fuel-stocks, soil- and livelihood-destroying monocrop plantations, and expensively capturing the carbon as smoke using toxic scrubbers that then have to be locked away somewhere forever].

As for the economic cost of a 40-70 percent emissions reduction, the scientists could not answer that other than to say it would be even more if we wait. The INDC pledges, they said, would not keep us to 2 degrees, but would lock in at least 3 degrees, probably 4. For northern latitude countries like Canada, Sweden and Russia, that equates to 6 to 8 degrees, which is unsurvivable by any measure.

Bottom line: the world is not on track to achieve a long-term survival goal for our species, but potentially successful means are available and must be scaled up urgently.

Bill McKibben, writing a short entry for a science fiction anthology, *Visions 2100 -Stories From Your Future,* to be released at the COP on December 5, said:

> Looking back on the century, the only real thought is: why didn't we do this sooner? The technology we're using - solar panels, windmills, and the like - were available in functional form a hundred years ago. But we treated them as novelties for a few decades - and it was in those decades that climate change gathered its final ferocity. Now we live in a low carbon world and it works just fine - except that there's no way to refreeze the poles, or lower the sea level, or turn the temperature back down to a place where we can grow food with the ease of our ancestors. Timing is everything, and it hurts to think we blew it.

Last year the International Energy Agency (IEA) presented an action plan that could stop the growth in emissions by 2020 at no net economic cost, reducing emissions by 3.1 GtCO2e (about 10%). They (incorrectly) claimed that reduction would be 80 percent of the savings required for a 2°C pathway.

Still, to follow the IEA's prescribed path, COP21 would have to recognize the need to fully decarbonize energy systems. Unfortunately, the wise men ultimately dropped the ball when they concluded in their SED report that "Carbon neutrality should be achieved in the second half of this century in the light of the limited global CO2 budget." This pushes the ambition standard at Paris well below where it will need to be.

One can only hope that someone will be allowed to fix that broken altimeter before the hard landing makes repairs moot. We only get one shot at this. Paris is it.

Timing is everything. Not only should negative emissions be allowed under the Paris regime, they should be mandated.

In September 2013, David Wasdell gave a talk to the Club of Rome[58] meeting in Ottawa entitled "Sensitivity, Non-Linearity & Self-Amplification in the Global Climate System" that ended with this slide, taken from NASA mission control during the Apollo 13 flight:

---

[58] The Club of Rome is a global think tank that deals with a variety of international political issues. Founded in 1968 at Accademia dei Lincei in Rome, Italy, the Club of Rome describes itself as "a group of world citizens, sharing a common concern for the future of humanity."

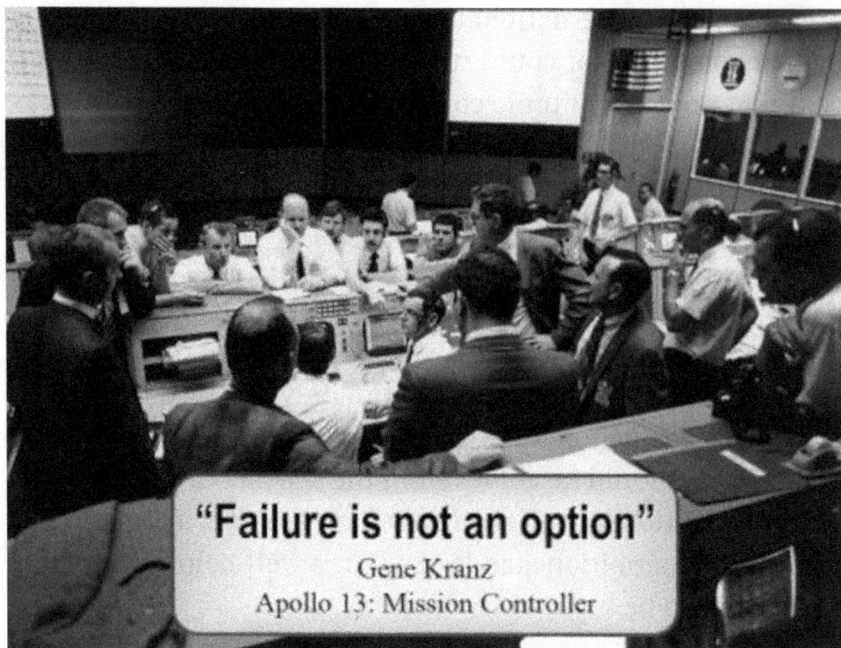

"Failure is not an option"
Gene Kranz
Apollo 13: Mission Controller

Paris: The Exposition

"What is immediately clear to everyone is that the sum of all pledges will not meet the budget."

In symphonic form, the second movement is Exposition. The usual tempo terms are *Andante* (slow), *Adagio* (slower), and *Lento* (slowest). This is where I find myself in the first week of the Paris Climate Summit. It is going from slow to slower.

The opening was grand and memorable, and although the popular press chalks that off to the French, and the World, standing tall against terrorism, it is really just how all COPs begin, with gala receptions from the host country, speakers congratulating everyone, digital fireworks displays, fine food, and live music. If the first theme is grand, the second is slower and lyrical - and in a different key.

In Haydn, Mozart, and early Beethoven, the entire Exposition is often repeated verbatim, to nail the themes down in the listener's mind. As often as not these days, the conductor will drop those repeats and just hope you buy the CD.

The opening sessions of the COP have the obligatory round of short statements by each member country, which is slow, repetitious, and sleep inducing after all the late-night parties. Tuesday has the official launch of work; resumption of the preparation of drafts for inclusion in the final document; and getting down to the nitty gritty of differences to be ironed out or papered over.

The opening statements were an interesting prelude to the coming drama for those versed in the "tells" of this kind of poker game. As Alden Meyer alluded to in his blog for the Union of Concerned Scientists after the Lima COP last year, there are many different ideas floating around about whom should shoulder responsibility for the cuts in standard of living that are implied by the scientific targets.

At COP17 in Durban in 2011, countries agreed that the post-2020 actions to be negotiated by next year's climate summit in Paris would be "applicable to all." To the U.S., other developed countries, and some developing countries as well, this phrase meant that the strict "firewall" between Annex 1 [overdeveloped] and non-Annex 1 [underdeveloping] countries would not continue in the post-2020 agreement; different countries would take on different kinds of actions, but those would be based on their capabilities and their current national circumstances, not by the binary division of the world in the 1992 Framework Convention.

However, other countries, in particular the Like-Minded Developing Countries group,[59] continue to insist that obligations in the post-2020 agreement must be based on the Annex 1 and non-Annex 1 groupings.

***

Norway calls for all countries to participate in the post-2020 regime, and sees a need to "differentiate according to the actual differences among Parties, and not on the basis of fixed categories of Parties." Norway says that it "would

---

[59] Members are Algeria, Argentina, Bangladesh, Bolivia, China, Cuba, Ecuador, Egypt, El Salvador, India, Jordan, Iraq, Kuwait, Indonesia, Iran, Malaysia, Mali, Nicaragua, Pakistan, Saudi Arabia, Sri Lanka, Sudan, Syria, Venezuela and Vietnam, representing more than 50% of the world's population.

expect all Parties with reasonable capacity and significant responsibility for global emissions" to put forward economy-wide emission reduction or emission limitation commitments.

Concentric Differentiation

In contrast to the Like-Minded group, which includes China and demands that the underdeveloping be permitted to continue underdeveloping as though this were the early 20th century, Brazil, joined by Mexico, has proposed an approach it calls "concentric differentiation," that would see all countries putting forward "quantified mitigation targets and actions."

Under concentric differentiation, overdeveloped countries would be expected to enact "economy-wide" reforms (a sneaky way to include the military) while the adamantly underdeveloping would be allowed sector-by-sector reforms. Naturally the US and UK are keen neither for a sharp line between North and South nor for starting to calculate their militaries' heating tab.

The Association of Independent Latin American and Caribbean countries (AILAC)[60] and the Least-Developed Countries[61] tend to fall into the pro-US position on this. While calling for the overdeveloped to sacrifice most, they ask for all to set ambitious goals.

Meyer predicted:

---

[60] Chile, Colombia, Costa Rica, Guatemala, Panama and Peru
[61] 34 countries in Africa, 9 in Asia, 4 in Oceania and 1 (Haiti) in the Americas.

Given the opposition of developed countries and of many developing countries to maintaining the Annex 1/non-Annex 1 groupings as the basis for obligations in the post-2020 agreement, it is clear that the position of the Like-Minded Developing Countries group is not viable. But the notion of purely self-determined obligations is not appealing to the vast majority of countries either; while it may represent the de facto basis for the first round of commitments under the Paris agreement, there will need to be more guidance in the agreement for subsequent mitigation commitments, as well as for the provision of finance, capacity-building, and technology transfer to developing countries, if it is to be acceptable to all. The submissions from Brazil, AILAC, Mexico, the Least-Developed Countries and others have much to offer in this regard.

What is going on now is the tallying of the commitment ledgers, reading through the INDC submissions of those that made their submissions and prodding those that have not. What is immediately clear to everyone is that the sum of all pledges will not meet the budget. Somewhere, somehow, deeper emission cuts in fossil fuels are required.

As if that order were not tall enough, there is a second fault line running through the negotiations that traces back to Hillary Clinton and the closing days of the Copenhagen COP in 2009. To get countries to switch from the binding treaty track to the voluntary pledge system, Secretary Clinton offered a big fat bribe. One hundred billion per year was the number she used. Oh, and a lot of whiz-bang new technology thrown in for the first 20 or so customers.

The Like-Minded Developing Countries insist that underdeveloping countries should only take climate mitigation actions if they get the finance and technology

Clinton promised. There is a fly in that ointment, and not a surprising one from what we remember of Clinton's days at the Rose law firm. It is in the accounting.

Show Me the Money

Last month the OECD issued a report concluding that wealthy countries have already made "significant progress" toward meeting their $100 billion a year promise. The report said that "climate finance" reached $52 billion in 2013 and $62 billion in 2014.

Apparently, I'm not the only one who can read a balance sheet. As the LMDCs are quick to point out, those numbers of $52b and $62b include market-rate loans that must be repaid with interest. They also include a lot of garden-variety foreign aid that is only marginally connected to climate change. True, everything is connected to climate, but does that mean humanitarian aid for war refugees should count as part of the $100 billion/yr Green Climate Fund? That number will certainly be going up this year. Will that count?

The Green Climate Fund, which came out of the Cancun COP in 2010, has so far received pledges amounting to about $10 billion, but only $1 billion has actually shown up, a dime on the dollar of what was promised. In November the Fund approved its first round - for 8 projects in Africa, Bangladesh, Latin America, and Fiji. The total for 2015 was $363 million.

It would be no small wonder if the LMDCs find more like minds during the COP in Paris. It is a bad omen because it sets in motion the selfish gene - "Sure, I will clean up your dirty greenhouse but you have to pay me" - when what is required for survival of the genome is selfless action on an unprecedented scale.

Selfless action on an unprecedented scale was the theme of the 3-minute address by President Obama. "[We want] a declaration that, for all the challenges we face, climate change will define the contours of this century more dramatically than any other." What will happen if we delay? "Abandoned cities; fields that no longer grow; political disruptions; conflicts; desperate peoples seeking sanctuary in nations not their own."

Obama said the US embraced its responsibility - as the world's largest economy and second largest emitter [elbow into the ribs of China] - to act, and called for unity among world leaders attending the talks.

> We must reaffirm our commitment that the resources will be there [in financial assistance for the developing world]. We must make sure these resources [of climate finance] fall to countries that need help ... and help vulnerable populations rebuild stronger after climate related disasters.

Union of Concerned Scientists, 350.org, and Climate Action Network called a press conference to express restrained support. Alden Meyer,[62] who has attended 20 of the 21 COPs, said Obama's change was representative of a larger shift in the member states. There is much greater awareness of dangers and costs of delay. Leaders of both overdeveloped and underdeveloping countries seem to understand both the existential nature of the threat and the economic challenge of addressing it. The math of the voluntary

---

[62] Alden Meyer is director of strategy and policy for the Union of Concerned Scientists and the director of its Washington, DC, office.

pledges adds up to less than what is needed, but it represents significant progress over the past.

This 2016 election will likely be the last in which the candidate of a major party is a vocal climate denier, Meyer said. The reason, May Boeve of 350.org said, is because until recently Big Oil ran the show. There has been a gargantuan shift in that power balance with the exposure of how fossil money corrupted the political and media processes within the United States. This has happened just in the past half-year or so, and one of the two major parties has been slow to recognize how much it has transformed the political landscape at the individual voter level. Polling shows the vast majority of people want fossil subsidies lifted and a rapid shift to renewable energy, and yet all the GOP candidates propose exactly the opposite. There is a disconnect there, that either will be corrected or cost elections until it is.

Meyer said the end of the fossil era was now inevitable. Decarbonization is coming. Whether you get with that program or miss the investment opportunity, you won't be able to stop it.

Laurent Fabius, the French foreign minister who is hosting the talks as COP president, said, "Future generations cannot hear us, but in a way they are looking at us now."

If they are even still there. Maybe we are speaking to an empty planet.

Paris Scherzo

"The Paris climate conference is really an economic conference, perched on the brink of a market crash in the fossil fuel sector."

Hanging out in the halls of Le Bourget, one often hears the phrase "the elephant in the room" in reference to unspoken but huge issues that may threaten the negotiations. In my view, the room is actually full of elephants, and it is a wonder delegates can even squeeze in to find their seats.

A new one that has made its appearance this year is the notion of measuring not merely a nation's consumption of fossil fuels (and presumably penalizing nations that consume more than they should) but also measuring production of fossil fuels (at the wellhead or mineshaft, *before* they are burnt).

This is a big deal.

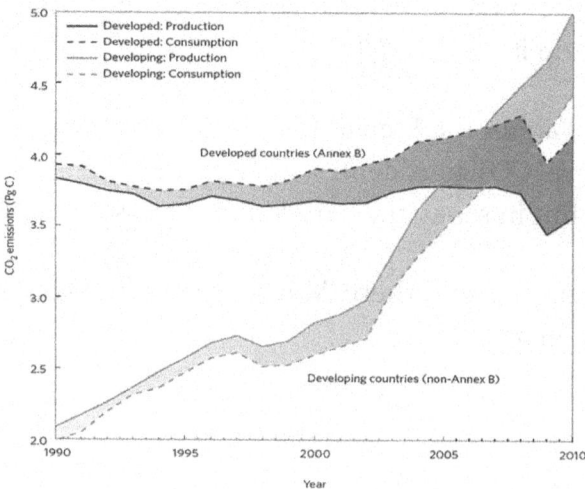

In a way it is not all that new, because I spoke of it in my book, *The Post-Petroleum Survival Guide and Cookbook,* back in 2006. My theme then was that production and consumption were two sides of the same coin; reducing consumption would also entail reducing production, but it was not necessarily a bad thing. Producing less could actually lead to a better life for people. My model was the dedicated beach bum who is content to work only enough to provide minimal needs and whose main products were serotonin and suntans.

In recent times I see more writers and thinkers coming to the same conclusion. I recently listened to an interview on the Kunstlercast[63] with Chris Martenson and Adam Taggart, authors of *Prosper! How to Prepare for the Future and Create a World Worth Inheriting.* To quote James Howard Kunstler's intro to the interview:

> Both Chris and Adam were corporate executives who dropped out to pursue a more resilient way of life in a rapidly and increasingly hazardous changing world. Chris Martenson began that phase of his career with the video and later book titled *The Crash Course,* which undertook to explain the dangers of contemporary banking, finance, and money-creation. Chris and Adam maintain the front and back ends of the PeakProsperity.com website, which features weekly articles and two excellent podcasts on issues pertaining to what I have called "The Long Emergency."

---

[63] kunstlercast.com. James Howard Kunstler's provides his weekly thoughts on the failures of modern urban design, suburban sprawl, American culture, peak oil, alternative fuel, the impoverishment of public places, and the tasks at hand to reform commerce, schooling, trade and agriculture in our civilization.

In *Prosper!,* Martenson and Taggert revisit my formula from the *Post-Petroleum Survival Guide* and also mention the recent book by two of our Gaia University graduates, Ethan Roland and Gregory Landua, *The Eight Forms of Capital,* that synthesizes the lessons of our Financial Permaculture Course in 2008, *et sequelae.* The outshoot is that if you think of your personal wealth and well being in strictly monetary terms, you are missing 88 percent of what life holds for you. Bringing this back to the climate context, scaling back from an overdeveloped, overextended civilization model to something more frugal can and should create greater satisfaction through the other forms of wealth.

Kate Raworth says:

> In Latin America they call it *buen vivir,* which literally translates as living well, but means so much more than that too. In Southern Africa they speak of *Ubuntu,* the belief in a universal bond of sharing that connects all humanity. Surely the English-speaking world - whose language has more than one million words - can have a crack at finding something equally inspiring. Of course this is not easy, but this is where the work is.

> Tim Jackson[64] has suggested "prosperity," which literally means "things turning out as we hope for". The New Economics Foundation - and many others - frames it as "wellbeing." Christian Felber[65] suggests "Economy for the

---

[64] British ecological economist and professor of sustainable development at the University of Surrey, author of *Prosperity Without Growth: economics for a finite planet* (2009), and currently the holder of the ESRC Professorial Fellowship on Prosperity and Sustainability in the Green Economy.

[65] Christian Felber coined the term Economy for the Common Good, now a social movement advocating for an alternative economic model. Note also the Schumacher Center for a New Economics, heir to the

Common Good." Others (starting with Aristotle) go for "human flourishing." I don't think any of these have completely nailed it yet, but they are certainly heading in the right direction.

This is, of course, a radical view compared to that held by most of the delegates in Paris. Petroleum, gas, and coal producers are not just multinational conglomerates like Exxon-Mobil - whom we have already heard squeal - but national producers like Saudi Arabia, Mexico, Brazil, Russia, Canada, and Australia. Mexico and Brazil are good examples of recently underdeveloping countries whose economies have boomed on the back of fossil fuel sales. In the desert kingdoms of the Middle East, few princes are willing to give up their palaces or swank townhouses in London for the sake of a few more degrees of heat, and the burn rate of Saudi royals' oil money has grown well beyond sustainable if those spigots were suddenly to close. Russia is fond of wielding the gas weapon when Europe or Ukraine get too snooty, and despite the good offices of Canada's new Prime Minister, do we really imagine Alberta will just shut down its tar sands?

Last week, Alberta's Premier Rachel Notley announced her province would enact a carbon tax, phase out coal-fired power plants, and regulate oil sands mining emissions. Those are wonderful promises, but not the same as leaving it all in the ground to begin with.

This argument over production places the producer countries, many of who are leading military powers, into conflict with their own internal balance of accounts. Earlier

legacy programs of the E. F. Schumacher Society founded in 1980 by Robert Swann. New Economics calls for cooperation for the social good instead of profit-orientation, greed and uncontrolled growth.

this year the UN's climate chief Christiana Figueres told the fossil fuel industry, "Three-quarters of the fossil fuel reserves need to stay in the ground." Mike Sandler at CapGlobalCarbon.com recapped the numbers:

> Three years ago Bill McKibben laid out the "terrifying math" behind the "excess fossil fuels," which if unearthed, would push the planet past the safe carbon budget as calculated by scientists. It starts with two degrees Celsius, the maximum level of acceptable temperature change that the world's nations agreed to above pre-industrial levels. From there, estimates of the world's remaining carbon budget vary depending on the level of acceptable risk. On the low end is McKibben's relatively risk-averse estimate of 565 gigatons (Gt) CO_2. A 2013 report from Carbon Tracker[66] put the number at 975 Gt for an 80% probability of remaining below 2 degrees C.

> The Intergovernmental Panel on Climate Change (IPCC) proposed a budget of 1000 billion tons (Gt) of CO_2 starting from 2011 that would give the planet a 66% chance of avoiding 2 °C warming. But Kevin Anderson of the Tyndall Centre for Climate Change Research[67] notes that between 2011 and 2014 CO_2 emissions from energy production amounted to about 140 Gt of CO_2, and when he subtracts emissions from deforestation and cement production through the year 2100 (60 Gt and 150 Gt), then at the current global rate of 35 Gt per year, the remaining 650 Gt would be used up in just 19 years! This puts the climate talks in Paris in perspective. There is no time for low initial national "contributions" with "ratcheting up ambition" after 5 or 10 year review periods. The entire carbon budget will be gone by 2034!

---

[66] carbontracker.org
[67] An inter-disciplinary research center dedicated to the identification, promotion and facilitation of sustainable solutions to the climate change problem. www.tyndall.ac.uk/

In our previous discussion of David Wasdell's work we indicated why the numbers Sandler is using here are too optimistic. The 2-degree guardrail provides no safety and even 1 degree is fraught with hazard. We need to get into net sequestration mode, ASAP, but the legal mechanisms for doing that are tricky.

Sandler suggests:

> If an outright ban is politically unfeasible and the goal is really to leave the fuels in the ground, then the global community must set an internationally agreed-upon limit that countries could sign on to, and to create an institution to regulate the budget under a declining permit system. This is the approach advocated by the group CapGlobalCarbon. The permits would be sold to the upstream fossil fuel companies, and the scarcity rent would be returned to the public as climate dividends. Representatives from CapGlobalCarbon[68] will be attending the climate conference in Paris, and will call for the creation of a Global Climate Commons Trust to set up a science-based permit system that follows the Cap & Share model. Whereas the UNFCCC is comprised of countries, the Trust would represent all of humanity on the basis of "one person, one share."

> The math is clear: there is a fossil fuel bubble. There is more coal and oil in the ground than we can safely burn. In this framing, the Paris climate conference is really an economic conference, perched on the brink of a market crash in the fossil fuel sector. The solution is to leave the fuel in the ground, and set up a price signal to allow a managed retreat from an obsolete industry, and protect the public by sending climate dividends back to households.

---

[68] capglobalcarbon.org

This is precisely the approach we advocated in July 2012 in our essay, "Toward a Unified Field Theory of the Elusive Kyoto Particle, or What the Green Party Might Learn from the Alaska Permanent Fund"[69]:

> The Alaska Permanent Fund can be seen as a successful example of a universal basic income - a natural resource dividend. It de-externalizes the price of nature - our primary economy in the final analysis. It makes it possible, by valuating pollution and depletion of limited resources, to save whales and glaciers. And it builds a buffer against hard times ahead when drill-baby-drill turns dry-baby-dry.

***

> We can stop injecting more by one of two ways: making it an international crime and enforcing sanctions; or putting a price on licenses to pollute and steadily shrinking the supply of permits, thereby gradually raising the price until only the most cost-effective projects can compete.

Recently George Monbiot[70] reached the conclusion that by not counting the production side of the ledger we were falsely congratulating ourselves for lowering our consumption by means of efficiency and other measures. This is a colossal hoax, Monbiot said, tantamount to accounting fraud.

> We can persuade ourselves that we are living on thin air, floating through a weightless economy, as gullible futurologists predicted in the 1990s. But it's an illusion, created by the irrational accounting of our environmental

---

[69] peaksurfer.blogspot.com/2012/07/toward-unified-field-theory-of-elusive.html
[70] monbiot.com/about/

impacts. This illusion permits an apparent reconciliation of incompatible policies.

Governments urge us both to consume more and to conserve more. We must extract more fossil fuel from the ground, but burn less of it. We should reduce, reuse and recycle the stuff that enters our homes, and at the same time increase, discard and replace it. How else can the consumer economy grow? We should eat less meat, to protect the living planet, and eat more meat, to boost the farming industry. These policies are irreconcilable. The new analyses suggest that economic growth is the problem, whether or not the word "sustainable" is bolted to the front of it.

It's not just that we don't address this contradiction. Scarcely anyone dares even to name it. It's as if the issue is too big, too frightening to contemplate. We seem unable to face the fact that our utopia is also our dystopia; that production appears to be indistinguishable from destruction.

Reaching out and welcoming the new elephant is a positive step, because that beast brings with it some very powerful solutions to our present dilemma.

Thursday, December 3, 2015

The Paris Bar Tab

"The bill is still considerably shy of being paid and the waiter is starting to look around for the manager."

During the pre-COP talks in Bonn, National Public Radio in the US ran a piece to explain the complicated negotiations. They compared the Independent Nationally Determined Contributions (INDCs) to a bar tab.

Lets say you have been in a bar a long time and a bunch of your friends have joined you. Some have been there as long as you have and others only just arrived. It is time to split the tab, so, like the INDCs, everyone throws some cash on the table. Someone has to take on the unhappy task of counting up the contributions, and in this case, they are quite a bit short of the bill. The waiter is standing there, looking impatient, and maybe expecting you to pull out your Diner's Club card.

If what has been put on the table were all to be paid, temperatures will go up by some 3.5 degrees Celsius this century without the full equilibrium calculation and at least double that at equilibrium. To get the settlement down to 2 degrees (by no means "safe"), we need more contributions, so you start asking everyone to chip in to the cash on the table. The US, Australia, and Canada, who were quite a bit short to begin with but have been there longest and drinking hardest, are a bit tipsy but feeling generous and decide to chip in more. China reluctantly joins them. India, who didn't put in anything yet, picks up a few hundred in cash off the table, saying it is owed for a previous tab. The bill is still considerably shy of being paid, and the waiter is starting to look around for the manager.

This raises some questions that are relevant to what is going on in Paris so we will carry the analogy a little further than NPR did. Firstly, who gets the honor of doing the count? Presumably there needs to be a UN office that does this, like the Green Climate Fund or some such. Some countries - most, in fact - are going to balk at being told what to do by some blue-helmeted One Worlders who want to take away their guns and impose some New World Order.

Secondly, what if it turns out the tab is wrong, by a sizable amount, as in fact it is? The barkeeper, in this case the Structured Expert Dialogue, comes around, all apologetic, and says, sorry for the mistake but you are going to have to pay much more than we indicated on the bill we gave you and here is the new bill.

Some of your drinking buddies turn out their pockets and say, we have no more, or rather, it would wreck our plans for the weekend. Call that the economics excuse. Some, the underdeveloping group plus China, say, "We only just arrived, this big tab is yours." Call it climate justice.

So now, if you really intend to pay this tab (don't even think what might happen if you don't, because then the Paris talks will be another bust and we are all screwed), you need to come up with a formula that everyone will agree to.

On the first negotiating day, Tuesday, the Overdeveloped Countries let it be known that the issue of "Loss and Damage" or climate justice, would not be part of the treaty. Those words were coming out.

That placed the proponents of the idea of historic responsibility, most notably India, on notice that these negotiations would not be patty-cake. The US would not be guilted in reparations for slave trafficking, the atomic bomb, or coal taken out of the ground before the Civil War. If India, or anyone else, wanted to be painted as the ones to stop the Paris Treaty, then they can go ahead and walk out right now.

So we see the lines being drawn. China and the Like-Minded Countries may need to back down on their insistence that Kyoto distinctions between the overdeveloped and the underdeveloping be retained. We are all in this together, and must hang together, or, to borrow from Benjamin Franklin, "we shall most assuredly all hang separately."

Climatologist Emeritus Jim Hansen, who had never attended a COP before, was induced to do a stand-up talk at Place 2B Tuesday night in which he pulled no punches. Calling the draft document "half-assed and half-baked," he said he sat down with UNFCCC head Christina Figueres a few months earlier and told her the same thing he is saying now, so no one should feel sandbagged.

Emissions reductions will not save us, if they are going country by country, based on a voluntary pledge system, Hansen said, because all you need to screw that up is for a few countries, like India, to say they do not feel a moral compunction to reduce.

Of the anthropogenic carbon now in the atmosphere, 25% is from the US, 25% from Europe, 10% from China, and 10% from India. The remainder is from everyone else.

Any reductions by the larger industrial countries would serve to reduce world demand for fossil fuels, which would make them cheaper, and then the outlaws and rapidly underdeveloping would consume even faster. If you put a carbon tax on all sources, Hansen told Figueres, you could avoid this, make the price global, and even keep it rising. The tax could be rebated to the public and most people would gain money (so-called "tax and dividend" or "cap and share"). The only ones actually paying more might be people with two houses or private jets. Figueres told Hansen a carbon tax would never fly, and "differentiated responsibility" has already been locked in.

I stopped by one of the booths belonging to a research institute working on clean coal. There are no technological barriers to removing carbon from the atmosphere, they told us. It's being done, and it works. You can capture carbon and store it. The barriers are strictly financial. If you want to change that, put a tax on carbon, they said.

The pub crowd here in Paris has not even agreed how to settle the bill, never mind how much to tip the waiter. Some are eyeing the exits and hoping to leave someone else with the tab, but no one has left yet.

Friday, December 4, 2015

Loss and Damage

"When water comes through your door it doesn't care if you are Republican or Democrat."

Climate conferences are always held in beautiful locations, and Paris is no different. If you tire of the gourmet bistros at Le Bourget, all of Paris is just a short metro ride away. In the evenings, when the weather has been as mild as it has been here in early December, the Parisian street cafés bustle with nightlife. If there was a horrible terror attack only a week ago, Parisians seem to have already forgotten. Besides, those casualties are but a small fraction of the number of innocents killed by rogue police in the United States each year, so let's put things in perspective.

Nonetheless, if you are anywhere in Europe, the refugee crisis will frame your story these days, and the COP-21 climate conference is no different. In the US, a clown version of politics seems to lead all news stories, and thus a story about the Senate passing a "binding resolution" pre-rejecting the Paris outcome by repealing the EPA's rules on power plant carbon pollution seems definitive, when in fact, even the average person here at Le Bourget will quickly tell you that the Republican bill passed with fewer votes than would be required to override Obama's veto (67) and so it really lost, not won. The EPA rules, and the forthcoming Paris deal, are alive and well.

What is emerging as a larger threat to the deal here is the issue of "loss and damage," which bears directly on the refugee issue and has very little to do with politics. Rain falls on the just and unjust. When water comes through your door it doesn't care if you are Republican or Democrat.

"Loss and damage" refers to the idea that climate change will affect different places more or less severely in any given year and what is needed is kind of a global insurance fund that can accept premiums from the entire world to help distribute the risk. Right now India is experiencing extreme floods and could use some help. Harjeet Singh, of Action Aid,[71] says India finds itself in a difficult trichotomy that makes everything worse. It is the third largest greenhouse gas polluter. Three million people have never had access to electricity but of course would like some, soon. And lastly, it has 7500 km (4660 miles) of coastline with massive vulnerability to sea level rise and flooding. On loss and damage, "We need progress by the end of the day today," Singh said.

Any insurance mechanism would also need to deal with "permanent loss," not just temporary catastrophes. Most of those refugees that are invading Europe from Africa and the Middle East are not temporary dislocations but permanent ones. Some left home for safety, and hope one day to return, but many, perhaps most in the future, will be leaving because entire regions have become uninhabitable. It is easy to list the kinds of permanent damage we can expect as temperatures rise and storms grow worse: loss of coastline, flooded plains, dried lakes, eroded slopes, rivers deprived of glacial meltwater, formerly fertile areas devoid of productivity.

---

[71] ActionAid is an international non-governmental organization whose primary aim is to work against poverty and injustice worldwide. actionaid.org

When the US threw down the glove and openly challenged the G77[72] on loss and damage, President Obama pointedly said they could not accept "unlimited liability." Moreover, one should bear in mind that Obama would need to ask Congress for funds - the US Constitution is quite clear who has the power of the purse - and if the US were made to pay a higher premium than others, whether for historical reasons or otherwise, that would be a non-starter for funding insurance premiums.

Still, after his session with India, Obama had a meeting with the Marshall Islands, representing the Alliance of Small Island States (AOSIS), 39 countries with the greatest sea level vulnerability, and smoothed the waters. "I am an Island boy," he told them. They laid out a very strong case for loss and damage, and he promised them the US would be willing to listen. Negotiating the details now shifts back to Secretary Kerry, Todd Stern and team, who will soldier on after Air Force One goes wheels up from Orly.

India, for its part, insists that any loss and damage provision must reflect "equity and differentiation," which are code for historical responsibility, and "ambition and means," which are code for "show me the money."

The drafters of the final document (in UNese, "ADP spin-off groups") are trying to find the least offensive, least contentious wording to slide over differences or defer hard choices. They are backloading ambition to 2020 and beyond. That carries a big risk because by not anchoring loss and damage in the Paris deal, it may mean the whole

---

[72] The Group of 77 (G77) at the United Nations is a loose coalition of developing nations designed to promote its members' collective economic interests and create an enhanced joint negotiating capacity.

insurance mechanism will never be enough to cover losses, at premiums anyone can afford.

Which causes me to lean forward for a tiny moment and stare into the abyss, before recoiling back and regaining my digestion. When the "loss" we are speaking of is of considerably larger magnitude than the shift of climate from any past ice ages to the present; when the scope of biodiversity loss, marine despoliation (hot, sour, and barren), and desertification are beyond any historical precedent, can we have any serious doubt that millions more will migrate?

Will it not become, as Lovelock predicted, huddled masses around the poles, hoping to survive?[73] What insurance plan can pay for that?

As I pass back and forth between The Place 2B[74] and Le Bourget by metro and shuttle bus, I am listening through ear buds to Kim Stanley Robinson's *Forty Signs of Rain* climate change trilogy,:

> Frequently, she found herself unable to concentrate, no matter her exhortations, and she would spend an hour or two digging around on the internet to see if she could find anything useful for Diane and Frank: old things that had worked but been forgotten, new things that hadn't yet been noticed or appreciated. This could be rather depressing of course.
>
> The government sites devoted to climate change were often inadequate. The State Department's page, for instance, began with the Administration's ludicrous goal of

---

[73] James Lovelock, co-author with Lynn Margulis, of the gaia theory (ecolo.org/lovelock), predicted this in *The Revenge of Gaia.*
[74] Place 2 B, St.Christophers Inn, 5 Rue de Dunkerque, 75010 Paris

reducing carbon emissions by 18% over ten years by
voluntary actions - a thumbing of the nose to the Kyoto
Treaty - that was still the government's only tangible
proposal for action.

Conference proceedings on another page spoke of "climate
change adaptation" - actually development agendas with
only a few very revealing admissions that "adaptation" had
no real meaning in regard to actual technologies, that the
whole concept of adaptation to climate change was a
replacement for "mitigation" and at this point, completely
hollow, a word only, a way of saying: "do nothing." Whole
conferences were devoted to that.

- Kim Stanley Robinson, *Fifty Degrees Below Zero*

Saturday, December 5, 2015

Kill All The Scientists

"We are being treated to the bizarre spectacle of an entire world of 195 countries held hostage by 60 or 70 millionaire Republicans in the US Senate."

We are reminded of Elisabeth Kübler-Ross's classic formulation of the stages of grief - denial, anger, bargaining, depression, acceptance - that are transferable to varying degrees and in different ways to personal change and emotional upset resulting from factors other than death and dying, such as the "solastalgia" distress produced by environmental change of one's home environment.

At the climate conference in Paris, denial has gained an upper hand over bargaining, as Saudi Arabia, speaking for (openly) the Arab States and (indirectly but transparently) for China, Russia, and Australia, as well as other oil- or coal-producing countries, has blocked the report of the Structured Expert Dialogue from reaching the floor of the plenary for consideration.

Barred were the 70 wise men's recommendations, such as discarding any notion that 2 degrees, or even 1.5 degrees, can be considered in any way safe, and leaving intact the fallacy that there are remaining parking spaces in the atmosphere that India and China can take their sweet time to fill by building more coal plants and fracking.

At a late-night session on Thursday, while several small committees took red pencils to a number of bracketed items on the negotiated text, striking items like adaptation finance (too "open-ended") and kickbacks for avoided deforestation, the Saudis objected to "anything of

147

substance" in the Structured Expert Review's being reported to the plenary.

To recap what we described here at the start of the week, the Structured Expert Dialogue was begun in 2013 and completed in 2015, released a report in draft in Bonn, watered down for presentation at the Summit, and then scheduled it for release here this week. Saudi Arabia drew its line in the sand and refused to back down. Procedural recommendations, such as periodic science reviews every five years beginning in 2020, were okay to mention. Just nothing of substance from the report.

After everyone had tried their best to get the Arab Group to back down, and the hour was drawing late, India and China sided with Saudi Arabia and so the deal was done. The COP-21 targets will not be based on science. Denial won the day.

The thing is, denial was already winning here in Paris. The debate over whether there could be a binding treaty signed, as has been promised since before Kyoto almost 20 years ago, is only necessary because the world's historically largest polluter, proud parent of 25% of anthropogenic greenhouse gas now heating the atmosphere, has a constitution that vests power over treaties in the hands of a Senate of 100 members, a hefty and safe majority of whom are millionaire climate deniers put where they are by the Koch brothers and other fossil money sources. And so we are treated to the bizarre spectacle of an entire world of 195 countries held hostage by 60 or 70 millionaire Republicans in the US Senate. Knowing they will never ratify a treaty forces all 195 countries to bend light around their star.

We are called *homo sapiens sapiens*, the smart, and now even smarter, variety of erect naked ape that diverged from other apes in the Pleistocene 2.5 million years ago. We got that name from Carl Linnaeus in 1758, but it may be overdue for an update. If the Holocene was our cradle, the Anthropocene is our assisted care facility. We have grown so demented perhaps we need to be straitjacketed so we don't hurt ourselves.

When I think of what sets humans apart from other animals, I tend to think of qualities like subjectivity, self-awareness, sentience, sapience, and the ability to perceive the relationship between oneself and one's environment. Many philosophers divide consciousness into phenomenal consciousness, which is experience itself, and access consciousness, which is the processing of the things in experience.

While we may yet retain our subjectivity, self-awareness, and communicative capabilities, we are steadily degrading our sentience, sapience, and perspective of just how far divorced we have become from the natural world.

That a small number of heads of countries who stand to personally profit in the extremely short term from kickbacks from fossil fuel industries can thwart an earnest and impassioned attempt by the majority of humanity to arrest climate Armageddon tells me that not only has the UN multilateral consensus process failed, but so have we all.

And so, like the Elves of Middle Earth, we pass into the west, taking our science with us.

Sunday, December 6

System Hacking

"Those countries that have become wealthy now have fertility rates that are below the replenishment level. And the reason these countries became wealthy is because they had energy, and that energy was fossil fuels. Unfortunately we can't continue to use that as the mechanism to get out of poverty."

- James Hansen

On this past Wednesday morning I decided to sit for breakfast with Stuart Scott, Founder of the United Planet Faith & Science Initiative (UPFSI.org), who was sitting by himself in the rear of Belushi's Bar at The Place 2B. I have been seeing Stuart since GEN's earliest forays into the world of the UNFCCC, also now being called the Climate Secretariat, when I was tracking the Committee on Sustainable Development and attending meetings of the CONGO, which is UN-speak for Congress of Non-governmental Organizations. Last December I featured Stuart's workshop on Arctic methane from COP-20 in Lima, Peru on my own year-end video mashup for our crowdfunding campaign. I asked him how he had managed to get Blue Zone passes for his guest speakers like James Hansen, Michael Oppenheimer, Kevin Anderson and Paul Beckwith.

"System hacking," he replied.

The UN system is complicated but if you have been doing it for as long as Stuart has, you know the codes, buttons and back doors. He explained that there was nothing abnormal about his methods, but rather that he had gained enough 'currency' with individuals and offices within the Climate Secretariat to accomplish things that might seem difficult to others less familiar. He also credits a lot of the metaphorical doors and windows he sometimes has to squeeze through to divine Providence. The name, 'Faith & Science Initiative' is quite intentional and sincere.

Stuart claims that his continual self-dedication to serving life on Earth allows him to ask for unusual things without shame or shyness. Having grown up in NYC does not hurt either. While GEN had struggled 6 months to get our plenary venue Side Event approved, he had bypassed almost the whole approval chain and booked a room for daily TV talk show presented as a press briefing under the banner of Climate Matters (climatematters.tv). Every day in Press Conference Room 3 there would be Stuart and his guests, web-streamed and simulcast to the UN system and COP-21 website and potentially millions of viewers, chatting about something that he felt was a critical piece of the puzzle that lay beyond what the conventional press was reporting about the climate negotiations, and the fundamental problem we are facing.

He invited me to stop in later and hear that day's briefing with James Hansen, one of the world's most famous climate scientists, who had until this year avoided all contact with the UN sponsored climate negotiations maintaining that governments were not talking about real solutions, but only about face saving solutions. Slipping into the back of a sparsely populated room, I watched Stuart do his warm-up talk. Most press briefings were not well attended and often they would be restricted to members of the press and delegates - I had only an observer badge. When it came time to turn to James Hansen, the room had filled and it was apparent that Stuart's hacking skills included knowledge that reporters are always a few minutes late.

Statement by Dr. James Hansen

COP21 Paris press briefing, December 2, 2015

Video on climatematters.tv. Edited transcript by Alex Smith, ecoshock.info, who also added emphasis.

The problem is that fossil fuels appear to the consumer to be the cheapest energy. They're not really cheapest because they don't include their full cost to society. They're partly subsidized, but mainly they don't include the effects of air pollution and water pollution on human health. If you child gets asthma, you have to pay the bill. The fossil fuel company doesn't. And the climate effects, which are beginning to be significant and will be much larger in the future are also not included in the price of the fossil fuels.

So the solution would be fairly straightforward. Let's add in to the price of fossil fuels the total cost - which you can't do suddenly but you can do it gradually over time, so that you can... people have time to adjust.

So I argue this should be done - and it has to be across the board, across all fossil fuels - coal, oil, and gas, at the source, at the domestic mine or the port of entry. And I also argue that that money should be given to the public, given equal amount to all legal residents of the country. That way the person who does better than average in limiting their carbon footprint will actually make money. In fact two thirds of the people would come out ahead. And it would also address the growing income inequality in the world, which is occurring in almost all countries, because low-income people would tend to have a lower carbon footprint. People who fly around the world and have big houses would pay more, but they can afford to do that.

That's a transparent, market-based solution, a conservative solution which stimulates the economy. The economic studies in the United States show that after ten years, if you had a ten dollars a ton of CO_2 carbon fee, distributed the money to the public - after ten years if would reduce emissions thirty percent. And after twenty years, more than fifty percent. And it would spur the economy, creating more than three million new jobs.

Furthermore, this is the only viable international approach. You cannot ask each of 190 countries to individually limit their emissions. What we have to do is have the price of fossil fuels honest. That requires only a few of the major players to agree 'Let's have a rising common carbon fee'. And those countries that don't want to have that fee, we'll put a border duty on those countries and furthermore we will rebate to our manufacturers that carbon fee when they export to a non-participating nation. This, economists agree, is a fair way to do it, and it could rapidly move us off of fossil fuels.

Stuart Scott: You've pointed out that if three major economies would do this all the rest would be forced to go along.

James Hansen: Well, almost all would go along because they would rather collect the money themselves rather than have us collect it at our borders.

But what we are hearing, is that although Christiana Figueres says many have said we need a carbon price, and investment would be so much easier with a carbon price, but life is much more complex than that. **So what we are talking about instead is the same old thing.** The same old thing that was tried in Kyoto asking each country to promise 'oh I'll reduce my emissions, I will cap my emissions, I'll reduce them twenty percent' or whatever they decide they can do.

You know, in science when you do a well-controlled experiment, and get a well-documented result, you expect that if you do the experiment again, you are going to get the same result. So why are we talking about doing the same thing again? I don't like to use crude language, but I learned this from my mother, so I'll use it anyway. This is 'half-assed' and it's 'half-baked'.

It's half-assed because there's no way to make it global. You have to beg each nation. So I went to Germany to speak with... I was hoping to speak to [Angela] Merkel but I got cut off at Sigmar Gabriel, the Minister. He said 'Oh, we're gonna do cap and trade, cap and trade with offsets.' And I said 'But that won't work, we've tried that.' So I said 'What's the cap on India?' And he said 'We'll tighten our carbon cap.' Well Germany is now two percent of the world emissions. So him tightening the German carbon cap is not going to solve the problem. You've got to have something that will work globally.

And it's half-baked, because there's no enforcement mechanism.... You know what I hear is all the Ministers are coming here, the heads of state, and they are planning to clap each other on the back, and say 'Oh we're really doing great. This is a very successful conference, and we're going to address the climate problem.' **Well if that's what happens then we're screwing the next generation, and the following ones.** Because we're being stupid and doing the same thing again that we did eighteen years ago.

Stuart can see Hansen has left an important foundation point out of his logical chain - when you give essentially the same remarks several times over the span of a day or two, take it from me you can easily forget what part of the story you have or haven't told. Stuart takes advantage of a pause by Hansen to bring in the missing point.

> Stuart Scott: You pointed out last night that if a large nation, even one nation, brings down its emissions with a cap, that also lowers the demand globally and brings down the price.…

> James Hansen: So what's the effect? You know you try very hard and you reduce our nation's emissions. Or an individual reduces their emissions. One effect of that is to reduce the demand for the product, and keep the price low. **As long as fossil fuels are dirt cheap, they will keep being used.** Burning coal is like burning dirt. You just take a bulldozer and you can bulldoze it out of the ground. It's very cheap but it does not include its cost to society. It's a very dirty fuel with some negative effects, which we now understand very well. We can't pretend that we don't know what's going to happen, if we stay on this path.

> This is the path we're on, you know. To pretend that what we're doing is having any effect... It might slow down the rate of growth, but that's not what's needed. Science tells us we have to reduce emissions rapidly. And furthermore, the economic studies show that if you put an honest price on carbon emissions, you would reduce emissions rapidly. But if you don't have that price on there, you are not going to reduce emissions. **You will reduce emissions some place, but then it keeps the price low, so somebody else will burn it.**

> Stuart Scott: And that economic study you are referring to also found that if you put ten dollars per ton, and increased it ten dollars per ton over ten years, what was the effect in jobs?

James Hansen: Well in the case of the United States economy, that's where the study was done in detail, it was three million new jobs in ten years and a significant increase in GNP [Gross National Product]. We need energy. But people thinking 'Oh, we have to do less...' - yeah we should have energy efficiency, but that would be encouraged by a rising price.

We do need energy. We need energy to raise the poor people out of poverty. That's the best way to keep population under control. Those countries that have become wealthy now have fertility rates that are below the replenishment level. And the reason these countries became wealthy is because they had energy, and that energy was fossil fuels. Unfortunately we can't continue to use that as the mechanism to get out of poverty.

We need clean energies. And the way to make that happen... You know, I've met with 'Captains of Industry' I call them - leaders of not only utilities but even oil companies. These people have children and grandchildren. They would like to be part of the solution. If the government would give them the right incentive, by putting this across-the-board rising carbon fee, they say they would change their investments and they could do it rapidly.

It's not that the problem can't be solved. But it's not being solved. And nothing that I've heard so far indicates that we're intending to ... it's not too complex. It's the simplest approach you could have: an honest, simple rising carbon fee.

And that was it, the 30 minutes had expired and the microphones were cut. Out in the hall and for the next couple of hours, reporters mobbed Hansen. He engaged in hard debate with them, baited them, asked them hard questions of his own. He was in his element, and now on an international stage with a receptive audience of the world press. He delivered an engaging counterpoint narrative to the '*Kumbaya*' mood at Le Bourget and stirred a controversy. Those ingredients make tasty media bytes.

He stayed until every one of them had their chance and wandered off to submit their stories satisfied with their engagement with this iconic scientist who has risked so much for so many years from his understanding of our predicament and his concern for future generations.

James Hansen came to speak truth to power, something he has been doing for more than 30 years. He has been censored, lost his funding, and at one point felt he needed to resign from his position at NASA, telling *The New York Times* that he could not both work for the government and sue the government at the same time. He has never wavered. While he may not have gotten what he might have hoped for, at least now he was being heard from the heart of the beast, the Conference of Parties.

Sunday, December 6, 2015

Taking Our Carrots to Paris

"Leave the sticks to others. We are carrot people."

If I had one do-over for my presentation at the Paris COP21 Climate Summit, it would have been to bring along a voice recorder so I could have a better recollection of my talk. Caught up in the moment, trying to make non-functioning audio, video, and Skype connections work, and quickly, the idea of recording slipped by. I have only what I can pull from my feeble memory, so here we go.

Sarah Queblatin, the Global Ecovillage Network's[75] excellent coordinator, introduced the panel and our humble network, then handed off to Geun Jeong of Green Korea, who showed some harrowing images of Korean children being scanned for fallout from Fukushima, but through slides, video and music, focused on alternative energy futures for her country, rising spontaneously from the grassroots. She handed off to Richard Siren and Lileana Lewinski of Asociación Proteger who spoke about their work in Argentina and Africa redesigning the built environment by recovering the native vernacular of natural buildings. We then brought in GEN President Kosha Joubert by Skype.

This is one part I really wish I had recorded, because Kosha's talk was marvelously comprehensive, taking us around the world to give the audience a taste of what might be possible if we could but pause and reason together. As the room filled with UN delegates from

---

[75] gen.ecovillage.org

around the globe, we glimpsed L. Hunter Lovins,[76] Dr. Tom Goreau, Benjamin Ruggill of Israel's Ministry of Environmental Protection, and many other familiar faces joining us. I can't include Kosha's slides in this book but fortunately she has co-edited a book to go with her talk, *Ecovillage: 1001 Ways to Heal the Planet* and that is well worth the purchase.

Then, as GEN's allotted time grew short, it was my turn to take to the microphone and give a rousing close about the weaknesses of the proposed treaty, the cost of 20-year delay, and the need now to go beyond zero and take more carbon from the atmosphere than is being emitted. "Emissions reductions will not save us now," I said, "but photosynthesis can."

I pointed to the sources and sinks, saying the atmosphere was passing its pollutants and heat to the oceans but the oceans were already overwhelmed. Only vegetation and soil remained as viable sinks. As climate warms further, as it must, they too will be stressed and absorption will diminish. Time is of the essence. I showed the slide from Exxon's recent report in response to Carbon Tracker calling for investigations into its stranded assets - the oil that could never come out of the ground unless we had a death wish for higher forms of life on this planet. Exxon, not surprisingly, maintained that the world will still be 85% dependent on fossil fuels in 2040. To underscore that conclusion, they showed images of a dark-skinned man driving a pair of oxen, leaving light furrows with his wooden plow as he planted a field, and a light-skinned man

---

[76] L. Hunter Lovins, author and a promoter of sustainable development for over 30 years, is president of Natural Capitalism Solutions, and the Chief Insurgent of the Madrone Project.

driving a modern tractor, leaving very deep furrows in his wake. The assumption was that any farmer in their right mind would quickly exchange the bullocks and handmade plow for the large-horsepower tractor.

Actually, I explained, that method of plowing is obsolete. It releases gigatons of greenhouse gases from the very place where we can still safely store them - in the soil. That style, which is still desertifying the most fertile foodbelts on Earth, is being replaced with a suite of tools that produce more food per land area and net-sequester more carbon every year, build soil, store water, and increase the resiliency of land to withstand storms, floods, and droughts. The new tools include no-till organic farming, agroforestry, aquaponics, keyline design, holistic management, remineralization, biochar from biomass energy production, and permaculture.

According to a recent report by the UN Commissioner on Human Rights, "ecoagriculture" is the *only* way we are going to feed the population of the world by 2040. Then we need to go beyond that and perform what Mark Shepard calls "restoration agriculture," building back the web of life and returning us to a garden planet.[77]

Here is just a quick example, taken from my ecovillage in Tennessee. We aerate a field with a keyline plow that raises the soil to let it breathe rather than turning it over. The shakers at the back of the implement drop biochar into the trench to permanently sequester carbon while providing

---

[77] *Restoration Agriculture* by Mark Shepard explains how you can have all of the benefits of natural, perennial ecosystems and create agricultural systems that imitate nature in form and function while still providing for our food, building, fuel and many other needs — in your own backyard, farm or ranch.

habitat for the soil food web. Compost tea, brewed just the night before, is carried at the front of the implement and injected at the root zone through drip hoses running the length of the plow shank. The tractor can be easily converted to run on either farm-brewed ethanol or biodiesel, depending on the engine type. Less than one percent of the field I showed would be adequate to supply the needs of that tractor for fuel, and it can come from waste products after the harvest is taken for food. Doing this every year adds 10 cm of dark horizon to the soil, and ten years of doing it builds dark earths, rich in microbial life and carbon, a meter or more deep. This can be, and has been done anywhere. The worse the condition of the soil when you begin, the more dramatic the recovery.

Biochar is so amazing you could almost call it magic rather than science. It is the secret of the terra preta soils of the Amazon. It is the quintessence of indigenous wisdom, nearly lost in the Columbian Encounter. After pyrolyzing[78] woody biomass, such as woody wastes after producing food and fiber, the charcoal takes on a crystalline form that remains in the soil for thousands of years. There are still remnants of biochars formed 400 million years ago in some places. This process, which can profitably co-produce food, energy, buildings, and other products, could take carbon that would otherwise reach the atmosphere and oceans as CO_2 or methane and safely convert the carbon for millennia-long storage deep in the soil profile.

I described a typical biochar cascade, acknowledging the work of Hans Peter Schmidt at the Ithaka Institute in

---

[78] Pyrolysis is a thermochemical decomposition of organic material at elevated temperatures in the absence of oxygen (or any halogen). See *The Biochar Solution: Carbon Farming and Climate Change* by this author.

Switzerland. I described the profitability of these approaches, building upon each other to provide yields at each step, rather than creating the necessity for massive subsidies, as in the case of "clean coal," to make the system function. Rube Goldberg inventions, like the kind Bill Gates is willing to fund, don't work. Healing is what nature knows how to do; you merely need to unleash that power and stand back.

A study of the Findhorn ecovillage in Scotland compared the ecological footprint of the UK and Scotland - energy, transportation, food production, industry, tourism, residential, etc. - to the ecovillage and found that Findhorn's footprint is less than half that of the national average. When you add in Findhorn's reforestation effort, Trees For Life in the Caledonian Forest, the village sequesters ten percent more than its footprint, and that number is growing. Earthaven in North Carolina sequesters 30 percent more than its annual footprint. The Farm in Tennessee, which manages 20 km² of forest, annually sequesters five times its own footprint.

I held up the Biolite Stove, which sequesters carbon while cooking your food, with no smoke, no ash, only biochar, and it produces electricity from the heat at the same time. I gave examples of how that technology was going to village scale in a variety of settings, using everything from Dorisel Torres' clay stoves[79] to 100 kW Power Pallets from All Power Labs.[80] I showed how in Kenya adding biochar made with clean stoves to the garden doubled the yield in the first season and made the crops much more drought- and pest-resistant.

[79] re-char.com/2011/03/28/new-possibilities-in-biochar-stoves/
[80] allpowerlabs.com/news/apl-receives-100kw-engine-for-100kw-gek.html

I spoke of our emerging business model - eCO2 - which uses social permaculture, indigenous wisdom, large-scale offsets for biodiversity, and multiple-ecovillage watershed economies to take all this to scale at the diffusion rate required to bring the planet back into normal Holocene range by mid-century. I spoke of some of the consequences if we did not, but I was more carrot than stick in my talk. We in the ecovillage world are carrot people.

I showed how Maslow's hierarchy of human needs is being degraded by climate change, but that with permaculture and ecovillages, we can reverse the process. Ecovillages are about designing our future as something we all want, rather than as something we are forced to accept in exchange for energy and commercial products. If we look at the hierarchy of human needs, we all want the same things, no matter where we live. Climate change, energy's hidden costs (such as resource wars), and population pressures are forcing us down the pyramid, to where simply getting enough food and water, or shelter, each day becomes our entire goal. Ecovillages move us in the other direction, while cooling the planet.

Ultimately we will need to find a way beyond zero. Carbon neutral will not be good enough. The two-degree goal will not be enough. The longer we take to curtail our use of fossil fuels, the more steep will be the decline required to get that legacy under control. If we start by 2020 and bring emissions down 6 percent every year, by about 2045 we still need to net-sequester carbon - we need to take more out of the atmosphere and oceans than we put in. We know now that for every degree of global temperature increase, the amount of methane being released from melting permafrost is equal to 1.5 times our current (2015) human emissions. At 2 degrees warmer, melting permafrost will still be emitting 3 times what we are today, even if we stop fossil extraction completely. So we have to get beyond zero and net-sequester. It is the only way. Putting it into the earth is the only safe and inexpensive way to sequester that much carbon, and ecovillages are showing the way, with style, enjoyment, and lots of good food.

I closed with two images: the first a supertanker, representing all the world's governments, trying slowly to change global policies, by consensus, from the top down; the second a shoal of fish, that could be just as large, moving just as fast, but capable of turning instantly and taking a new direction. This is what ecovillages bring to the climate discussion.

We are not speaking of what might be, with some conceptual planning document, untested in the real world. We come to the United Nations from 20 years or more of actual work on the ground. We are strong enough now to be reaching out to help in emergencies, with refugees, and with rebuilding after disasters. We do that from bases of power, not from fragile seeds or laboratory experiments.

Today, in this time, in these places, we bring optimism and real hope, not because it might be done but because we are doing it. Ecovillages are better places to live. They show a path to the future where life, although consuming far less, is better. In most cases it is vastly better than everything else around. We are here because what looks to many as the end is for us only the beginning. We have ambitious plans, not merely for ourselves, but for humanity, the forests, the oceans, and the earth. This is how it will be done. This is the only way it can be done. And we are doing it.

Drums Along the Seine

"When we are told the hoop is broken, this is the meaning. It is not difficult to understand."

Some years ago, in an essay for my blog I described the ordeals I undertook in search of extrascientific cures for the seemingly intractable imbalance of climate. I would always ask the spirit guides to point me towards some easy way out of the climate catastrophe ahead, but I never felt answered. At least I took some balm to heal my own disabling ennui from this isolating knowledge we all must soon share.

At the 2009 COP-15 I roomed at Hildur Jackson's farm, just outside Copenhagen, with an Estonian Kriya yogi, a Buddhist priest, one of founders of Auroville in India, an African aid worker, an Irish diplomat, and Maurice Strong, who only recently passed, just before the start of this Paris summit.

Maurice was one of our guides - "sat gurus" - in this life's strange odyssey. Maurice was Founding Executive Director of the UN Environment Program and not a believer in summits as an end in themselves. Rather than setting up his UNEP shop in Paris or New York, he established a global headquarters on what was then a coffee farm at the outskirts of Nairobi. Maurice was Secretary-General of the UN Conference on Human Environment in Stockholm (1972) and the Rio Sustainable Development Summit (1992), and he launched both the UN Framework Convention on Climate Change and the Convention on Biological Diversity.

His partner Hanna invited two Asháninka shamans to Hildur's farm and one night convened an impromptu ceremony, which was, for me, overpowering and awe-inspiring. While I have yet to experience a vision of universal peace and harmony through international law, as I would love for the Abuelita to provide, I still persist in this long winding path that seems to have been laid out for me and continuously marvel at the places it goes.

And so it was, when I received a late night call from Helen Samuels, Ambassador of the Choctaw Musgokee Yamassee Nation, to join the elders at a prayer ceremony on the Seine, I did not hesitate. Parenthetically, let me say that The Farm ecovillage in Tennessee, where I have lived since 1972, inhabits a small 20-square-kilometer portion of former Choctaw Musgokee land, on Swan Creek upstream from the Singing River, so when summoned by our esteemed landlord I would only naturally go out of respect. Which is not to say we do not respect mysterious guidance at any time, whether in the call of an unusual bird, a voice in my head bearing the words of departed ancestors, or a messenger from our plant allies - there are no coincidences.

At the Seine, I met Jane Goodall's Paddle-to-Paris contingent of original peoples and boarded a river cruise boat with them for refreshment and relaxed conversation.

There I was joined by many old friends of like guidance, squished alongside ecovideographer John D. Liu, Greenpeace founder Rex Weyler, and later Sail Transport founder Jan Lundberg. As the boat slipped its moorings and moved out into the current, the elders began a ceremony to join our minds and purposes.

On deck were the Four Worlds International Institute, Embassy of the Earth, Fundaçion Cuatro Mundos, Front Siwa Lima, Salish Sea Foundation, Netherlands Centre for Indigenous People, Compassion Games International, UNO Foundation, Choctaw Musgokee Yamasee Nation, Ihanktonwan Dakota Treaty Commission, Brave Heart Society of Ihanktonwan, Consejo de Visiones-Guardianes de la Tierra, Tsleil Waututh Nation, World Conscious Pact, and the International Council of Thirteen Indigenous Grandmothers.

"Science confirms the warnings and prophecies of our wise ancestors and elders," said Chief Phil Lane Jr., Ihanktonwan Dakota and Chickasaw Nations. "Our new vision is, in fact, an ancient vision. We must leave the destructive path that has created these global challenges, and walk the life-enhancing, principle-centered path of protecting and restoring the Human Family, our future generations, and our beloved Mother Earth."

As we passed beneath the Eiffel Tower, the amazing bridges of Paris, Grand Palais, Petit Palais, Louvre, Les Invalides, Cathedral Notre Dame, Conciergerie, Place de La Concorde, Palais de Chaillot, L'Assemblée Nationale, Musée d'Orsay, and Institut de France, there was a steady drumbeat, the scent of burning sage, and prayers.

I had the sense, however, that I was not at a healing ceremony, rather a funeral. The drums beat a dirge.

When I spoke at Le Bourget the day before, I provided the antidote to the poison, and it had been a gift from these people, the ones on the boat. It had cost them 100 million souls, or many times that. It was the gift of good land. It was the ability to make soil, to take nourishment and then to give back; to close the circle.

When our ancestors speak of the sacred hoop, this is it. The closing of a circle. When we are told the hoop is broken, this is the meaning. It is not difficult to understand. You can call it shamanic, or magic, or superstition, but this simple story has kept us alive for millions of years and in close families with our relations, through many ice ages, and even a few periods of significant warming. The Haudenosaunee refer to this as the original instructions, given to us by the Creator. When we built our cities, stopped sharing, locked up the food and medicine, and forgot where it all comes from, we lost our instructions.

In journeys like this, the original instructions reappear. We can choose to take them home with us, or we can forget them again. It is always a free-willed choice.

Tuesday, December 8, 2015

The Coal Tumble

"The television news on any night is like a nature hike through the Book of Revelations."

-Al Gore

Over in the business gallery, on Investors Day, Carbon Tracker hosted a side event called "Investing for the Long Term: Addressing the Carbon Asset Risk," which was a rollout for the report called "The $2 trillion stranded assets danger zone: how fossil fuel firms risk destroying investor returns."

Anthony Hobley, Carbon Tracker's CEO, said,

> The financial system is a complex ecosystem. When you really start to drill into it and understand where the pressure points are, the influence points, there's a lot of them. The credit rating agencies are important, and we've done a number of joint reports on S&P, so to be fair to them they are starting to understand this issue, and particularly the S&P have done a number of reports around the credit risk in coal. And, boy is there credit risk around coal.

> If you look at our US coal equities case study, 80 to 90 percent of share value lost in 5 years. Considering when that study was done the numbers would be much higher now. Eighty-six US coal companies have gone into chapter 11. If that is not a financial meltdown within a particular sector I guess I don't know what is.

> Regardless of what happens in Paris we are in the middle of a technological transition to a low carbon economy. The

technology, in many ways, is in the driver's seat. What we are about here in Paris is the policy signals; how quickly that shift is implemented. Is it implemented quickly enough to keep us below the 2 degrees?

The shift underway is impressive even without the meltdown of the fossil industries. "In the last six years," said Hal Harvey, CEO of Energy Innovation, a policy research group, "solar prices have dropped by more than 80 percent, and now cost less than a new coal plant. Wind is down 60 percent, and LED lights more than 90 percent." With other new technologies near at hand "it becomes clear that a clean future costs no more than a dirty one."

Moreover, the lines are crossing. Renewables prices are falling fast while fossil extraction costs climb. Both are exponential curves, the former driven by innovation and Moore's law,[81] the latter driven by inexorable physical depletion rates.

This does not stop politicians from putting a thumb on the scale at the urging of their fossil masters, the wealthiest companies and countries on Earth. Fossil fuel companies enjoy 40 times the government beneficence bestowed upon renewables. While renewables can outbid for contracts against new fossil fuel plants on a level playing field, that field has long been tilted to favor non-renewables. Fossil fuel plants built before the current regulatory era, without any pollution control, and with all their capital expense amortized and still enjoying subsidies, can run very cheaply - if you don't count their damage to public health and the

---

[81] "Moore's law" is the observation that, over the history of computing hardware, the processing power of the solid-state integrated circuit has doubled approximately every two years while the cost of production has halved.

global commons. New nuclear, coal and gas plants are almost never competitively bid.

The night before, we had dinner with Jan Lundberg and Charlene Capro of the Sail Transport Network. Sail transport is a good example of retrofuturism - how we can gracefully transition from an impossible reliance on a self-destructive energy source back to something akin to the way we were developing before, but way cooler than what we used to use.

It was not that very long ago that goods were transported over the globe by sail power. The first "coal war" was probably the Spanish American War, which used the pretext of a steam boiler explosion aboard the Maine, anchored in Havana harbor, to seize strategic coaling stations in Guantanamo Bay and the Philippines. Nobody ever had a war over wind resources.

The Sail Transport Network came to Paris concerned about maritime shipping emissions - which have been in and out of the new agreement, depending on which day of the week this is. The International Maritime Organization, which the Kyoto accord vested with authority to regulate this sector, has long failed to acknowledge UN climate goals as part of its mandate, so a large part of the greenhouse gas inventory continues to come from the unrestricted burning of dirty bunker fuel, and annual emissions are growing, not shrinking. If shipping were a country, it would have the same greenhouse effect of Germany. Total emissions from just the 15 largest ships (the kind that carry automobiles) equal all the automobiles in the world in soot, lead and noxious pollutants. The obvious, clean alternative is sail technology.

Jan and Charlene were in Paris to change this state of affairs. STN and its sister organization SAIL MED are following up on an European Commission project's outreach to 26 nations regarding sail technology as a form of renewable energy that can be funded by the UN and the EU. The project, SAIL consortium, had by June 2015 finished design of the Ecoliner, a hybrid sailing cargo ship designed by Dutch naval architects Dykstra, that offers massive energy efficiency gains and zero emissions under optimum sailing conditions.

"The people who harness 'free fuel' will be the energy tycoons of the future," said Diane Gilpin of B9 Shipping and the Smart Green Shipping Alliance. Gilpin is developing a 100 percent renewably powered, commercially and technically viable sailing hybrid cargo ship to be commercially viable today and future-proofed for a 30-year lifespan. Simultaneously, there is rapid growth in the use of traditional sailing ships, with opportunities for young sailors of all nationalities to see the world from the top of a wooden mast.

Former Vice President Al Gore was asked to keynote the event and he delivered a rousing call to battle.

> One of the dramatic differences in the reality that we are living in, in these days of the Paris conference, compared to previous conferences, is that the business community, investors, technology developers, researchers and others have brought the technologies of solar photovoltaics and windpower and efficiency in a variety of different forms and battery storage and sustainable forestry and sustainable agriculture to the point where these new approaches are extremely competitive with the legacy approaches that we are quite used to.

Just today Goldman Sachs Energy Group put out another study that said that the extra energy additions to the world energy economy from 2015 through 2020 from solar photovoltaics and onshore wind will be as large as all of the additions to the world energy supply from natural gas, chiefly fracked gas, between 2010 and 2015. ...

We saw the best estimates for the advancement of wind energy back in the year 2000 predicting that by 2010 the world would add 30 GW of wind. We exceeded that projection by 12 times over. Two years later, in 2002, the best available predictions were that the world would add 1 GW of solar electricity per year by 2010. That goal was exceeded by 17 times over. Last year it was exceeded by 48 times over. This year it will be exceeded by more than 62 times over. That's an exponential curve.

It is not only the exponential cost down curve associated with renewable energy which is having such a powerful impact - an impact that was unexpected by so many - it is also the nature of it; it has zero marginal cost. The next kilowatt-hour is free, once your solar and wind is in place. That's what led TXU, one of the investor-owned electric utilities in the state of Texas to introduce its new rate plan for its customers in Texas.... It tells its customers, "From 9 pm at night to 6 am the next morning, use all the electricity you want, for free."

"For free."

South Australia has had electricity for free. Several other regions of the world have already begun to adapt to the new realities of zero marginal costs. This also creates a vicious cycle for carbon-based electricity producers because the up-time each day for those facilities declines dramatically. When you have a choice between paid and free, the choice is usually free.

The difference between zero degrees and one degree in the weather is a difference of more than one degree. It is the difference between ice and water. The difference in markets between 'more expensive than' and 'cheaper than' is similarly a non-trivial difference. The explosive growth in demand, once that threshold of 'cheaper than' is crossed, is quite remarkable. And we are seeing that threshold crossed now in region after region all over the world.

Will companies react? Depends on whom you ask. The panel got a question from a financial trade reporter who pointed out that most pension analysts, never mind the companies themselves, were not stress testing for the effects of climate change, stranded assets, or divestment movements.

Hobley responded:

The problem we have with incumbents, and this is not just the fossil fuel companies - this has happened again and again in business history. Incumbents almost without exception fail to survive technological transition. The Kodaks of this world, you know, Blockbuster - if you come from the U.K. at one point there was a Blockbuster on every corner - and the steam locomotive manufacturers. If that was not true, the car you drive would be built by the people that used to build steam locomotives. The camera in your phone would be built by Kodak and you'd be streaming your videos from Blockbuster.

So why is that and how can we make that different this time? If we don't get those companies to change, a lot of value is going to be destroyed and our analysis shows that to be the case. So how do you get those companies to transition? One of the critical things is you have to insure on the boards there are people who are not part of that group think.

Divestment[82] - this is the most powerful movement since the anti-apartheid movement and in many ways since the civil rights movement in the United States. It has cut through like no other. So how do we build on that and get the mainstream in the financial markets to react?

There was really no answer to that question, but one thing was for certain. A very large change is in the air.

Here in the business pavilion at Le Bourget I could detect a lot of deep inhales.

---

[82] gofossilfree.org

Down to Business

"If you manage billions of dollars, pounds, rubles, or euros of your own or other people's money, it has by now not escaped your attention that it is all at risk in a most profound way."

I have to confess I tend to cast a jaundiced eye whenever I see proposals to save the planet through the power of business, free enterprise or so-called "fair trade." My first instinct is to make sure my wallet is still there.

A dogged protest has stalked nearly every COP since Kyoto, unfurling its banners with slogans like "System Change not Climate Change." The protest has found an unlikely ally in Pope Francis, whose *Laudato Si* encyclical pointed the finger at capitalist greed and made it inseparable from the climate crisis. Naomi Klein's latest bestseller, *This Changes Everything,* is a critique of capitalism and a call for citizen "blocadia" to stop the gears of destruction. The protesters and the Pope are providing grand and spirited gestures and speaking undeniable truths, but we have to wonder whether making a Paris agreement dependent on the dawning of the Age of Aquarius is a viable strategy.

That said, I sense a sea change in business as usual. When Henry David Thoreau said it was no good having a comfortable house if you did not have a habitable planet to put it on, he was not referring to posh villas overlooking Cannes or infinity pools on private islands in The Seychelles. And yet, for the upper one-tenth of the one percent living in such places, he may as well have been. It took a while, but now they get it.

If you manage billions of dollars, pounds, rubles, or euros of your own or other people's money, it has by now not escaped your attention that it is all at risk in a most profound way.

The IPCC's (vastly overestimated) atmospheric budget of 1,000 $GtCO_2$, even with highly optimistic assumptions on curtailing deforestation, air travel, shipping, and cement emissions, requires global reductions in CO_2 equivalence of at least 10% each year, beginning as quickly as possible, transitioning rapidly to zero emissions by 2050 and then going beyond zero. The severity of such cuts would likely exclude even clean coal and natural gas from most countries' energy mix after 2025, President Trump's Energy Policy Task Force notwithstanding.

Reality cannot be reconciled with repeated claims by world leaders and renewables advocates that in transitioning to a low-carbon energy future "global economic growth would not be strongly affected." *You know that is not true!* You cannot grow an industrial economy on daily sunbeams the way you can from 500 million years of stored sunlight. Heck, you can even send people to the Moon on the kind of energy we've been getting from dead dinosaurs. But there are only so many of them down there, and they are getting harder to find. (I am being flip, by the way. Dinosaurs came much later in evolutionary record than the biota that bequeathed us our coal and oil).

Late one afternoon, as I was packing up to leave for a dinner and sake with Sail Transport Network's Jan Lundberg at a sushi place just off the Rue de Dunkerque, I noticed Alden Meyer rushing down the hall towards me. He was trying to catch up to an entourage of high-net-worth individuals wearing suits tailored in Hong Kong that were just then entering Observer Room One. I asked Meyer where he was going and he pointed to the room and said, "Fireworks."

I followed along and took a seat towards the back of the room. The side event was called "Charting a Low-Carbon Course for the US Power Sector." At the dais, checking their mikes, were Brian L. Wolff, Executive Vice President, Public Policy and External Affairs at Edison Electric Institute (a fancy title for a lobbyist, the former legislative aide to Nancy Pelosi, Robert Matsui, and Rahm Emanuel), PG&E Chairman and CEO Tony Earley, EEI President Pat Vincent Collawn, and EPA Administrator Gina McCarthy.

It was easy to see what Meyer had been referring to. One of the Obama Administration's most contentious recent moves was to put strict new standards on carbon dioxide emissions from steam plants making electricity from coal, the main "base load" for most of the United States. The standards were actually not all that strict - 1400 lbs. CO_2 per megawatt-hour was still permitted, even in new plants. The regulations, however, developed under the 1970 Clean Air Act, outraged Congress and were forced to endure a Supreme Court challenge. Earlier this year, a separate regulation, to limit mercury, lost a 5-4 decision at the high court, but the power plant carbon dioxide rules survived.

If anyone expected fireworks between the electric utilities industry and the EPA Administrator, Gina McCarthy, they were disappointed. "People think of us like Dan Aykroyd and Jane Curtin" (comic news commentators on "Weekend Update" in the 1980s - "Jane, you ignorant slut!"), she began, "but it is far from the truth.""

Between McCarthy and the other panelists there was no separation. Each of them in turn described cost savings, investment returns, and job growth from not merely the new Obama clean air regulations but the massive switch to green energy that was all the buzz at Paris. The energy transition is already happening, they said; renewables had come down 50% in cost while coal and fracked gas investments are tanking. To oppose that perfect storm was foolhardy. The electric utilities were on board and letting out sail rather than tacking into the gale.

All of this green energy talk is refreshing but we need to remember that human civilization is a heat engine. It needs to be completely reversed if anyone is going to survive. Degrowth may be unmentionable in Paris, but it is the only policy that gives us any chance to survive to the end of this century. Tyndall Centre's Kevin Anderson observes:

> ... [T]here remains an almost global-scale cognitive dissonance with regards to acknowledging the quantitative implications of the analysis, including by many of those contributing to its development. We simply are not prepared to accept the revolutionary implications of our own findings, and even when we do we are reluctant to voice such thoughts openly.

At a side event on Tuesday called "Growth, the Driver of Climate Change Action," presented by Brazil, Climate Policy Initiative, and Brookings,[83] Sir Nicholas Stern mentioned four ways to move towards the zero or negative emission rates that will be necessary: soil rehabilitation; reforestation; CO_2 capturing from the air; and biomass with carbon capture. He said that economic decline from

[83] The Brookings Institution is a nonprofit public policy organization based in Washington, DC.

resource overshoot and population pressure, notably migrants from South to North, would likely mean that governments would not be up to the task.

He did not mention the historically unprecedented 200-trillion-dollar debt bubble that has been blown up in financial markets since 2008 and is now hovering like a balloon over the world economy.

Stern's prognostication was affirmed at the Press Briefing on Wednesday by US Secretary of State John Kerry, who, after posturing for some 20 minutes, pulling out every platitude imaginable about the heroic work we are all undertaking and how this will be humanity's finest hour - "... our commitment to the global clean energy economy that every one of us knows we need if our future is to be secure..." -finally slipped in some statements worth picking my head out of my chest for.

> Ladies and gentlemen, the situation demands, and this moment demands, that we do not leave Paris without an ambitious, inclusive, and durable global climate agreement.

> Today we are formally announcing, the United States, that we are part of what we are calling the "High Ambition Coalition." ... Addressing climate change will require a fundamental change in the way that we decide to power our planet, and our aim can be nothing less than the steady transformation of the global economy. And that's not a pipe dream, some sort of pie-in-the-sky idea that's way out there and we're waiting for Godot to come along and give us the answer. That's not it. This is not a situation where we have to hope and pray that some smart person is going to come along and find a solution. No! We already have the solution!

Remember, one of the things that we expect to happen here and makes Paris so important is not that we're going to leave here knowing everything we do is going to hit the 2-degree mark, but what we are doing is sending the marketplace an extraordinary signal, that those 186 countries [that submitted INDCs] are really committed. And that helps the private sector move capital into that, knowing that there is a future that is committed to this sustainable path. That is why we need a strong, legally binding, transparent system.

The High Ambition Coalition that Kerry blew the cover on has been gathering in secret for 6 months. It consists of 79 African, Caribbean, and Pacific countries, the US, and all of EU member states. Notably absent are Australia, South Africa, Brazil, China, and India. The Canadian delegation, ebullient with the replacement of Stephen Harper by Justin Trudeau, only just joined.

The group is focusing on at least four key issues. They want an agreement at Paris to be legally binding; to set a clear long-term goal on global warming that is in line with scientific advice; to introduce a mechanism for reviewing countries' emissions commitments every five years; and to create a unified system for tracking countries' progress on meeting their carbon goals.

- Karl Mathiesen and Fiona Harvey, *The Guardian*[84]

On Tuesday the group demanded a binding agreement with five-yearly reviews to consider more ambitious targets for the world and individual countries. They wanted clear rules for all countries to report on their emission reductions promises and have them reviewed and revised.

---

[84] theguardian.com/environment/2015/dec/08/coalition-paris-push-for-binding- ambitious-climate-change-deal

That piqued oil-rich Saudi Arabia, Venezuela, and Malaysia - who complained of procedural irregularity and argued the talks should revert to line-by-line negotiations. India said flatly it did not intend to revisit its promised emissions reduction target until 2030.

Hewlett Foundation President Larry Kramer said that new technologies cannot drive change by themselves because of inadequate regulatory frameworks. Neither can climate finance philanthropy provide the needed scale of resources for the necessary investments. Kerry said the overdeveloped countries could not go it alone and even if they reduced all emissions to zero tomorrow, the Earth would continue to warm without comparable cuts coming from the Two-Thirds World. So where does that leave us?

As we looked out the windows at French robocops manhandling journalists who strayed too close to the Grand Palais, we had to say it would not come from street protest. It had to come from the direction Kerry was pointing - *the Illuminati!*

The Illuminati

"A good tactic is one your people enjoy. They'll keep doing it without urging and come back to do more. They're doing their thing, and will even suggest better ones."
                                        - Saul Alinsky, *Rules for Radicals*[85]

Despite the grand claims by Bill McKibben and Naomi Klein that public protest had brought down the Keystone pipeline and transformed energy utilities, we seriously doubt that. What stopped the pipeline is the same thing that stopped King Coal: the economic downturn in China driving the price of crude oil down; the halving in the price of renewables despite a half century of every possible barrier and disincentive being erected by the Department of Energy, the White House, and most governments around the world; and, not inconsequentially, some gnome bean-counters in Switzerland actually running the numbers and closing the spigot on fracking and tar sands, as they must eventually on genetic modification, not because of health concerns, but because they are scientific and economic frauds.

The smart money wants to go green, fast. Jean-Dominique Senard, CEO of Michelin, said pointedly, "You should never oppose the future."

Michael Bloomberg was equally succinct: "No CEO could survive if they said climate change is not a problem." Leading companies are seeing an average 27% internal ROI on low-carbon investment.

---

[85] Saul Alinsky was a political activist and writer generally considered to be the founder of modern community organizing.

If the Illuminati[86] actually exist, they have suddenly, after a quarter century of heel dragging and backsliding, had a come-to-Jesus!-the-climate moment. They have realized the existential implications of climate change and are altering the marching orders they are sending to their minions. This is a moment of what Naomi Klein coined as "disaster capitalism." Fossil fuels are the great disaster and the captains of finance have a secret plan all lined up to seize the moment.

An example of that is "We Mean Business," a consortium of 353 companies, with $7.2 trillion in revenue and $19.6 trillion under management, 50 of which have already committed to 100% renewable energy (RE100). WMB has an 8-fold demand for the Paris treaty that sounds like it could have been written by Climate Action Network:

1. NET ZERO GREENHOUSE GAS EMISSIONS WELL BEFORE THE END OF THE CENTURY

2. STRENGTHEN COMMITMENTS EVERY FIVE YEARS

3. ENACT MEANINGFUL CARBON PRICING

4. NEW AND ADDITIONAL CLIMATE FINANCE AT SCALE

5. TRANSPARENCY AND ACCOUNTABILITY TO PROMOTE A RACE TO THE TOP

6. NATIONAL COMMITMENTS AT THE HIGHEST END OF AMBITION

7. ADAPTATION TO BUILD CLIMATE-RESILIENT ECONOMIES AND COMMUNITIES

8. PRE-2020 AMBITION THROUGH WORKSTREAM 2

---

[86] The Illuminati ("enlightened") is a name given to several groups, both real and fictitious. Historically, the name usually refers to the Bavarian Illuminati, an Enlightenment-era secret society founded in 1776.

The Portfolio Decarbonization Coalition (PDC) is a multi-stakeholder initiative that aims to cut greenhouse gas emissions by having institutional investors (*i.e.:* the owners of trillions of dollars of assets) redirect their capital to low-carbon investment opportunities. For 2015, PDC set a target of decarbonizing $100 billion in Assets Under Management. In November it announced it had smashed its target, hitting $230 billion.

The take-home point for Parties in Paris is that while they haggle over a few missing billions in government and private contributions to the Green Climate Fund they are losing sight of the trillions that can be unlocked with the keys already in their hands.

The French Environment Minister Ségolène Royale announced a global call for tender to create cheaper and more efficient electric vehicles. The goal, she said, is to produce EVs that can be sold for less than €7,000 (usd$7600), with a charging time of 30 minutes and a 500 km capacity. That carries a number of implications. To bring down the cost, designers will have to use fewer, cheaper, and 100% renewable resources. Think molded bamboo frames and biochar fuel cells made from banana peels.

Anthony Hobley, CEO of Carbon Tracker, said that a critical element for remaining within the limits of a habitable Earth is the need to pull back from projects in the "danger zone." He pointed to billions of dollars tied up in projects that are simply not needed due to massive cost reductions in renewable energy technology and changing demands. The US has the greatest financial exposure with $412 billion of unneeded projects, followed by Canada

($220bn), China ($179bn), Russia ($147bn), and Australia ($103bn).

Solar and wind are already getting to grid parity across the globe, and earlier this year, Warren Buffett set a price of three cents per kilowatt hour for his 100 MW solar farm.

ING, a Dutch investment company, announced this week in Paris they will stop financing new coal-fired power plants and mines worldwide and will turn away new clients whose business is more than 50 percent dependent on coal.

As the final days of COP-21 draw to a close, the divides are familiar. Dropping the goal from 2° to 1.5°C above pre-industrial levels now seems within reach. Not the temperature - that is no longer within reach - but the Maginot Line[87] and the effort to defend it.

Those resisting this goal, such as India, China, and the Arab States, suggest that such a target would represent too heavy a burden on competitiveness, economic development, and poverty alleviation. The US, Australia, and Canada have switched sides and are backing 1.5 to stay alive.

On the issue of finance, underdeveloping economies - those that are transitioning from agriculturally secure, renewably based societies to overpopulated consumerist fossil-addicted client state Ponzi systems - require enormous capital to invest in new coal plants, super-highways and

---

[87] The Maginot Line was an "impenetrable" border of steel and concrete fortifications erected by France after World War I, at considerable cost. The line was defeated in less than one week in 1940 when Germany simply went around it by violating the neutrality of Belgium, Luxembourg and the Netherlands, and flew over it with the Luftwaffe.
187

megacities they'll need to pursue unobtainable economic growth and customer population expansion that exists only in their dreams. Dozens of countries have aspirations like this and have sent delegates to Paris to push for their Bollywood fantasy of curry in every pot.

On the other hand, overdeveloped countries grappling with financial collapse from years of officially sanctioned systemic ripoffs and lagging resource extraction from the edges of their empires are struggling to meet Hillary Clinton's commitment to mobilize $100 billion per year in support of the bribes extorted at Copenhagen.

While other important differences exist, these issues are the biggest impediments to success at Paris. They are slowing the pace of negotiations and undermining trust. Some countries seem intent on rejecting reasonable compromise because they fear being economically disadvantaged or thrown off their projected growth trajectory, as if that were even possible for anyone but unashamed economists.

What could shift the argument might be private sector investment, within an enforceably defined regulatory regime, with accountability and transparency, to deploy low-carbon and net-sequestering technologies, including biomass-to-biochar carbon capture and storage with agriculture and ecosystem service benefits. These represent an investment opportunity pegged by Stern and others at $4.7 trillion. For Ponzi economists it is a wet dream, and for red-eyed French diplomats trying to bring this puppy home, it is God-sent.

A few countries seem intent on making requests that cannot be met and are well beyond the bargaining range - what negotiators call pozo, the "zone of possible agreement." Include India, Bolivia, and Saudi Arabia as asking for "nozo." Continuing to push for impossible positions risks everything for nothing.

We Mean Business writes:

> The climate action plans tabled by national governments in the run-up to COP21 are already on course to change the temperature trajectory from an estimated 4.8°C by the end of the century to an estimated 2.7°C. Is that enough? Not at all. But a thriving clean economy and a platform for further ambition is contained within those INDCs. Moreover, for those looking for climate finance, remember, the deal itself is the financial package. The combination of a long-term goal, an ambitious review mechanism, appropriate mechanisms for transparency and accountability, and seed capital for low-carbon development provided by the public purse creates the environment for trillions of dollars in investments and funds the innovation that will drive our common success."

In his famous 1971 *Rules for Radicals*, Saul Alinsky said, "A good tactic is one your people enjoy. They'll keep doing it without urging and come back to do more. They're doing their thing, and will even suggest better ones." In this case, anyone who wants utilities to get off coal or nuclear power should look up and see if there are solar cells or a windmill on their house and maybe a bicycle in the shed and complimentary currency in their pocket.

Alinsky warned, "The price of a successful attack is a constructive alternative. Never let the enemy score points because you're caught without a solution to the problem.... Pick the target, freeze it, personalize it, and polarize it." This is what is happening to the street protesters outside the corporate venue, who are having their lunch eaten by Big

Business as it mashes the accelerator on the green technology revolution.

When engaging in a large-scale political conflict involving civil disobedience, Gandhi believed that satyagrahis ("truth warriors") must undergo training to ensure discipline. He wrote that it is "only when people have proved their active loyalty by obeying the many laws of the State that they acquire the right of Civil Disobedience."

Gandhi contrasted satyagraha (holding on to truth) with duragraha (holding on to force) by saying the latter was meant more to harass than enlighten opponents and change the status quo. He wrote: "There must be no impatience, no barbarity, no insolence, no undue pressure. If we want to cultivate a true spirit of democracy, we cannot afford to be intolerant. Intolerance betrays want of faith in one's cause."

One of the biggest roadblocks to achieving the Paris treaty, after Senate Republicans in the US, is India. India demands $2.5 trillion in development pledges before it will implement its national commitments to carbon reductions put forward by its government ahead of the talks. Moreover, it is intolerant of any agreement that will force it to cut its high-carbon development path before mid-century, bending the science to fit its politics.

Secretary Kerry said,

> We did not come to Paris to create a ceiling that contains all we ever hope to do. We came to Paris to build a floor, on which all of us together can continue to build. The progress that we've made, particularly with respect to INDCs, is unprecedented and encouraging, but it alone

will not be enough. The targets that we've announced, taken together, will make a major dent in global emissions. They will bend the curve. But they will not hold the temperature to 2°C, which is what scientists tell us is what needs to happen to prevent the worst impacts, or lower than that, even, if possible, the 1.5, whatever. And that is why it is important that we keep an eye on our targets and ensure that they are as ambitious as possible, that we understand whether we are making progress, that we set up a system to review our targets and ratchet them up at regular intervals if we need to, and given the rapid pace that I just mentioned, in which technology is evolving, in five years the individual capacity of one nation or another could increase dramatically.

Both Wednesday and Thursday will have midnight sessions, it was announced this afternoon by COP President Laurent Fabius. Delegates hope Friday will be a day of rest while the legal and linguistic group reviews the text. The next iteration of the text, expected for Thursday afternoon, will be what Fabius calls the "penultimate text." We shall see. Some brackets are more stubborn than others.

Governments may not be able to curb India's counterambitions. But maybe the Illuminati will, especially if, like ING, they refuse to do business with anyone who leaves Paris and is still burning coal. That would be most in keeping with the spirit of the Mahatma.

As we ride the shiny new hybrid electric green bus back to the Paris Metro, past shops lit with bright Christmas displays, I am once more listening to the *Forty Signs of Rain* trilogy piping through my ear buds.

The President's team continued to transpose what was working for Chase into the President's campaign. They began to proclaim the bad weather to be an economic opportunity of the first order. New businesses - even entire new industries - were there for the making. The bad weather was obviously yet another economic opportunity for market driven reforms. However, since he had been elected with the help of big oil and everything transnationally corporate, and had done more than any previous president to strip mine the nation and use it as a dumping ground, he did not appear to be as convincing as Phil. It was beginning to be a bit hard to believe his assertions that the invisible hand of the market would solve everything because, as Phil put it, the invisible hand never picked up the check.

- Kim Stanley Robinson, *Fifty Degrees Below*

Friday, December 11, 2015

Paris: Top of the Stretch

"What is missing from last night's draft, in my view, was strong, coercive language."

Things are starting to move in the Paris talks. The energy in the halls of Le Bourget is palpable. Nonetheless, we are starting late. We have waited too long to get to here. We have poked the hornet's nest with a stick. Next, we have to run. Dr. Guy McPherson puts this is into its larger context:

> Astrophysicists have long believed Earth was near the center of the habitable zone for humans. Recent research published in the 10 March 2013 issue of *Astrophysical Journal* indicates Earth is on the inner edge of the habitable zone, and lies within 1% of inhabitability (1.5 million km, or 5 times the distance from Earth to Earth's moon). A minor change in Earth's atmosphere removes human habitat. Unfortunately, we've invoked major changes.

This discussion, although doubtless included in the briefings being given almost weekly to President Obama by his science advisor, John Holdren, seemed strangely absent in Paris, placed at the margins into side events from the IPCC, Met Office, Hadley Centre, Yale University, and others. Sure, the countries of the world rallied to thwart Saudi Arabia, India, and others' efforts to subvert the 1.5°C goal. Nor were the obstructionists permitted to dump the provisions on transparency and uniform accounting, although it was not for lack of effort.

But still, we keep hearing reference to an outdated and unfortunate IPCC number - the bent straw everyone is grasping for - that to have a 50-50 chance, or 66% chance, of limiting warming to 2°C (itself untenably overheated), cumulative emissions to end of century and beyond must be limited to 1 trillion tons of carbon dioxide in total, starting 5 years ago. In that past five years, we burned through one-tenth of that sum - 100 Gt. Most predict that with added growth (a big assumption) we'll have burned through 75% of this "budget" by 2030 and we'll bust the budget around 2036. If we cut back, we might have until 2060.

One of the briefings I attended at Le Bourget was by the Met Office, one of England's top climate research laboratories. Those scientists, in subdued, unemotional language, completely shredded the notion that we have another ten years or any amount of time left to keep pumping carbon into the atmosphere. They also reminded delegates the permafrost that is now melting contains more than 1400 GtC and is quite capable of putting all of that amount, more than the entire inventory of fossil emissions since the first oil wells were drilled 150 years ago, into the atmosphere in a fortnight.

It is as yet too soon to know how this story will be told a century or more from now.

One version is that by then, owing to the methane clathrate gun, the Atlantic Current, or some other nasty self-reinforcing feedback, Earth resembles Tatooine, the desert homeworld of Anakin Skywalker, his son Luke, and the Jedi Master Obi-Wan Kenobi. The planet is oppressed by harsh deserts and only a small portion remains that can sustain life, and that is shrinking. In this scenario, the story of COP21 in Paris is meaningless. We were genetically not predisposed to do what we had to do to survive, methane concentrations will eventually eliminate mammalian life, and so there is not much of a future ahead for us.

A somewhat different story might be that although the changes wrought by sudden onset climate change have been drastic, erasing most coastal cities and taking us past 2 degrees, they have not stopped human ability to ingeniously adapt by moving underground, planting drought-hardy forests to cleanse the atmosphere, and abandoning inhospitable regions. Population is inching down, partly by the severity of the weather but increasingly by a popular will to live more in balance with what nature can provide. In this scenario, what happened in Paris was clearly inadequate and tone deaf, and most people will sneer or spit when it is mentioned.

A third possibility is that life is actually a bit better in 2115 than now. Sure, there are still lots of hazards to be wary of, like superstorms and extended droughts, or that nasty Fukushima disaster no one has yet figured out what to do with, but 2015 was when the world decided to use the last few drops of fossil sunlight to make an aggressive switch to solar energy and permaculture, and now ubiquitous windmills made of bamboo composites and low-tech solar thermal devices perform enough useful work for everyone that leisure time can be devoted to philosophy, reading and writing books, making music and art, and social networking.

This world of the future also has common threads with Tatooine, in that something like a race of Jawas - actually, tribes of gleaners and scavengers - travel about in pedal-powered sandcrawlers collecting scrap metal and plastic bits from worthless consumer junk from failed industrial projects. In this world, the events in Paris a hundred years earlier are looked upon as a sort of turning point, when the arc of human history swung away from self-destruction and relearned to garden.

Then, of course, we have the heavy metal sci-fi version subscribed to by Bill Gates, Elon Musk, and most of the political leaders in Paris today, which involves shiny nuclear plants, test-tube food, towering megacities filled with well-fed workers that live to be 200, and colonies on Mars. Grow grow grow! This scenario is, of course, fiction unless someone suddenly discovers an energy source comparable to fossil fuels, which seems implausible because no one has - but that's a fortunate break for the many species not already driven to extinction by human ecosystem expansion.

It is really quite amazing how much unjustified optimism is floating around this climate discussion. Earlier in the year Elizabeth Kolbert attended an event hosted by the French government at the Miami Convention Center titled "Eyes on the Rise." In the December 21, 2015 *New Yorker* she quotes the response of Miami Beach Mayor Philip Levine to the threat of sea-level rise:

> I believe in human innovation. If, thirty or forty years ago, I'd told you that you were going to be able to communicate with your friends around the world by looking at your watch or with an iPad or an iPhone, you would think I was out of my mind. Thirty or forty years from now, we're going to have innovative solutions to fight back against sea-level rise that we cannot even imagine today.

So, dwelling on that third story, the green energy one, sitting around the fire in 2115, what do we think? We imagine the obvious question a child might ask is why ever did they wait so long? We could have done this long before and there would still be polar bears and whales and we would not have these unpredictable monsoons and droughts. Were they that oblivious, the child asks, or was it willful? We would have to say it was a little of both.

In countries like the US and Australia, where corporate control of media and fundamentalist legislation of school curricula dictate what people know about most things, the climate threat was ridiculed and silenced. Even in Paris nearly every speech by a USAnian began by apologizing for being scientific and not as ignorant as the average US citizen, Republican or otherwise, just as nearly every speech by a European somewhere made reference to the tidal wave of refugees. Climate was always filtered through political rose-colored glasses, no matter where you were. Because of that, people seldom saw the world the same, or got anything close to an accurate view of what was really happening. The colored glasses made you oblivious, but you always had a choice about whether to take the glasses off.

They only had to turn off their televisions and walk outdoors, we might tell the child. "What's a television?" she might reply.

The truth is, those few who correctly diagnosed the situation early were labeled Cassandras, anarchists and flakes. You would not find much mention of them in popular news media, except for the occasional derisive reference. In 2115, those people are heroes.

Most of yesterday the arguments continued around Le Bourget on the points of contention we have been describing all week. The document scheduled for 3 pm release was delayed to 7 and then 9. When it was finally issued there was a two-hour period permitted for review. Each country was rationed 3 badges, no more, for the final "indabas" (Zulu for agreement circles) begun at 11:30 and going much of the night. Each topic of contention was given its own space and a skilled facilitator. This morning we are awaiting the "final" text that the indabas have agreed to and the coordinators have synthesized.

From the near-final text last night, it seems agreed that 1.5 degrees is in the treaty, not as a mandate but as a defense line, as the Structured Expert Dialog had urged. It first appears in the Preamble, which says, "consistent with holding the increase in the global average temperature to well below 2°C above pre-industrial levels and pursuing efforts to limit the temperature increase to 1.5°C, recognizing that this would significantly reduce risks and impacts of climate change...."

It next appears in Article II, the voluntary pledge protocols, where the document notes with concern that existing pledges will not deliver 2° and that "much greater emission reduction efforts ... will be required in the period after 2025 and 2030 in order to hold the temperature rise to below 2°C or 1.5°C above pre-industrial levels[.]" Article II concludes with a call for the IPCC to provide a technical paper by 2018 on the likely impacts of exceeding 1.5 and the required emissions pathways to hold the line there.

The Guardian's John Vidal observes:

> Many of the ambitious plans to cut emissions submitted to
> the UN depend on up to $1 trillion being made available to
> invest in renewable energy, farming and forestry. This
> money is not available and will depend on flows from new
> carbon markets and other uncertain financial sources. In
> addition, only $57 billion of the $100 billion pledged to be
> "mobilized" by rich countries to help poor countries adapt
> their economies to a warming world has been identified.
> Because developing countries have had long experience of
> failed promises and pledges they are not going to roll over
> without financial guarantees. They fear double counting
> and the diversion of aid flows, and although they will fight
> hard for money they will meet rock-hard resistance from
> the rich, who are determined to commit as little as
> possible.

Loss and damage provisions are back in, mandating a
review in 2016 to develop "modalities and procedures for
the mechanism's operation and support." Adaptation is back
in, but largely locally driven, with financial support from
the Green Climate Fund. Finance is made contingent upon
"enhanced results-based payments for verifiable achieved
emission reductions and removals related to existing
approaches...," which is to say nobody gets a free lunch.

Needless to say, nowhere in the four corners of the
document is reference made to agriculture (although food
security is raised as a concern for adaptation purposes),
biochar, holistic management, soil fertility, mob grazing, or
planting new forests for carbon sequestration. There is no
mention of ecovillages, transition towns, or permaculture,
although the section on adaptation does make mention of
empowering community-based solutions, driven by
transparent, egalitarian processes, and that is laudable.

What is missing from last night's draft, in my view, was strong, coercive language. A striking example is in removing fossil subsidies, where countries are *urged* "to reduce international support for high-emission investments." Why not just require that? Words like "takes note," "requests," "invites," and "urges," need to be replaced with words like "shall," "must," and "are required."

A good example is a particularly strong paragraph 111, where the body:

> *Decides* that the committee [facilitating implementation and compliance] ... shall consist of [X] members with recognized competence in relevant scientific, technical, socio-economic or legal fields, to be elected by the Conference of the Parties ... on the basis of equitable geographical representation, with [X] members each from the five regional groups of the United Nations and one member each from the small island developing States and the least developed countries, while taking into account the goal of gender balance.

That committee is a key part of the agreement, because they will be influential in what happens next. In the legally binding treaty part, Article II.2 says:

> The committee shall be expert-based and facilitative in nature and function in a manner that is transparent, non-adversarial, and non-punitive.

There are no sanctions, no fines, no punishments, and no leverage that can be applied to enforce the treaty. There is not even something like the ING decision to not do business with anyone relying more than 50% on coal. No boycotts, trade sanctions, tariffs, fees. The treaty is based entirely on trust and voluntary compliance.

What the treaty does fairly well is set ambitious but not impossible goals and suggest ways to achieve them. You can quibble about whether the ambition is strong enough, but this is a big first step, and more steps will follow. The first "global stocktake" is set for 2018, with subsequent reviews and revisions every 5 years.

We will soon find out what the outcome of all the overnight indabas was and how much has changed.

Last night, I was passing an outdoor café and was hailed by my friend Daniel who wanted to know what our take on the talks was. "Are we f**ked?" he asked.

"Not yet," I replied, and although I meant that we still have another day or two of negotiations ahead, in a larger sense here we are, sitting in an outdoor café, enjoying peak civilization as though nothing has happened. And yet, in a larger sense the world has changed completely, and yes, we really are f**ked, although there may never have been much we, who were born this late in the game, could have done.

For the grandchild, there is even less she can do; just hope and wait. The hope is that it is not already too late and that the puny start we are making is at least leading us in the right direction. And that was better, to quote Keats, "than if I had stayed upon the green shore, and piped a silly pipe, and took tea and comfortable advice."

Kiss the Ground

"Food security and combating climate change are complementary; regenerative practices that store carbon in the soil have the potential to cool the planet while ending world hunger."

While the world focused on a deal to reduce emissions, another international initiative was quietly signed at the Paris climate conference, highlighting a critical but seldom-acknowledged climate solution: soil.

In a standing-room-only crowd of 300+ delegates, French Minister of Agriculture Stéphane Le Foll announced the 4/1000 Initiative, pledging to increase the organic carbon level of agricultural soils by 0.4% per year. France had obtained pledges from over 25 countries – and would bring that number to 50 during COP-21 – as well as hundreds of food, agriculture and research organizations.

The "4/1000 Initiative: Soils for Food Security and Climate" is a voluntary action plan launched after COP-20 under the Lima-Paris Action Agenda, backed by an ambitious research program. It aims to show that food security and combating climate change are complementary; that regenerative practices that store carbon in the soil have the potential to cool the planet while ending world hunger, despite the expected new stress of rapid climate change.

"This is the most exciting news to come out of COP-21," said Andre Leu, president of IFOAM - Organics International. "By launching this initiative, the French government has validated the work of scientists, farmers and ranchers who have demonstrated the power of organic regenerative agriculture to restore the soil's natural ability to draw down and sequester carbon." It positions farmers as the pioneering climate heroes of the next generation.

While soil was not on the official agenda at the climate conference in Paris, the representatives from an informal coalition of soil organizations brought the topic to the masses at a number of panels and side events, and from the Eiffel Tower itself. "The conclusion is simple," said Minister Le Foll. "If we can store the equivalent of 4 per 1000 (tons of carbon) in farmland soils, we are capable of storing all man-made emissions on the planet today."

"We're spreading the 'aha' moment of our lifetime," says Ryland Engelhart, California restaurateur and co-founder of Kiss The Ground. "Healthy soil is a solution right under our feet."

Food writer Michael Pollan, in a *Washington Post* Op-Ed on December 4th, wrote:

> Unfortunately, the world leaders who gathered in Paris this past week have paid little attention to the critical links between climate change and agriculture. That's a huge mistake and a missed opportunity. Our unsustainable farming methods are a central contributor to greenhouse gas emissions. Climate change, quite simply, cannot be halted without fixing agriculture."

***

"Some scientists project that 75 to 100 parts per million of CO_2 could be drawn out of the atmosphere over the next century if existing farms, pastures and forestry systems were managed to maximize carbon sequestration. That's significant when you consider that CO_2 levels passed 400 ppm this spring. Scientists agree that the safe level of carbon dioxide in the atmosphere is 350 ppm.

Marin County ranchers have found that applying a single layer of compost, less than an inch thick, to rangelands stimulates a burst of microbial and plant growth that sequesters dramatic amounts of carbon in the soil - more than 1.5 tons per acre. And research has shown that this happens not just once, but year after year. If the practice were replicated on half the rangeland area of California, it would sequester enough carbon to offset 42 million metric tons of CO_2 emissions, roughly equal to all the CO_2 emitted by the State's electric utilities each year. Adding an inch of compost to all the rangelands each year would sequester as much as electric utilities, residential and commercial emissions combined.

What is being left out of that calculation by the good people at Kiss the Ground are the big gorillas in California's emissions picture: the industrial sector (77 million metric tons) and transportation, most notably the freeway system (200 million metric tons). California would need to convert its deserts to rangelands to get that much carbon locked away every year.

Kiss the Ground also glosses over the difference between labile and recalcitrant carbon. While compost stimulates soil organisms and that moves carbon down from the surface into the root zone for longer sequestrations, most compost decomposes closer to the surface and emits greenhouse gases in the process. That is just the labile carbon cycle, get used to it.

The recalcitrant carbon cycle - biomass to biochar - locks carbon up for thousands to millions of years. Still useful to stimulate the soil biology, it has the added benefit of holding more oxygen and water, which better mitigates the damage of extreme weather. By combining compost with biochar, the California story could become one of negative emissions - net sequestration - almost immediately, continuing indefinitely.

That would be a story worth taking to the world, and fortunately it was, by Cornell soil professor Johannes Lehmann and agroforestry colleagues in a Side Event in the Africa center, by Guy Renaud and the team of ProNatura[88] at the exhibitions in the Grand Palais, and by Jim Mason and Silvia Sandri showing the AllPower Lab's Cube biochar pyrolysis at the Gallery of Climate Solutions at Le Bourget.

And one night, the Eiffel Tower joined in, lighting up the image we show on the cover of this book, with the words, "The Soil Story."

---

[88] ProNatura is tackling the social, economic and environmental problems that face rural communities in the underdeveloping world. The aim is to provide viable economic alternatives to those people struggling to make a living from imperiled environments.

Friday Night, December 11

Place 2B

We need a revolution in means, not only a revolution in ends.

On Friday night, while the indabas haggle over the final text, our hostel transformed into its nightly "Place to Brief." Special guests included Fanny Benedetti,[89] Charles Eisenstein, Bruce L Erickson,[90] Valérie Mahdjouba,[91] Estelle Le Touze,[92] Jean Viard,[93] and Amy Goodman, host of *Democracy Now!*[94]

Weary COP delegates and activists wandered into Belushi's Bar, made their way to a staircase leading down, and descended into the basement cave below Paris, outfitted as a sound stage, where the nightly performance was live-streamed to a world audience. Taking seat in folding metal chairs, our GEN team joined in listening to our French hosts interview the guests.

I was most interested in what Charles Eisenstein had to say, although I have read his books, *The Ascent of Humanity, Sacred Economics,* and *The More Beautiful World Our Hearts Know Is Possible,* and shared the occasional speaking platform with him. In my view the hosts did not let him speak enough to flesh out his points, so I will instead report here some comments he posted to an

---

[89] Benedetti is a founding member and executive director of the French National Committee for UN Women.
[90] Futurist, writer, speaker and international management consultant. brucelerickson.com/
[91] Author and filmmaker.
[92] A founder of Grandparents for the Climate.
[93] Research director at CEVIPOF , Centre de Recherches Politiques de Sciences.
[94] www.democracynow.org

internet discussion earlier in the day, warming up to his talk, that expanded on what was said that night. He said:

I think there are deep problems with the standard climate change narrative, which has equated "green" with carbon reduction. One obvious problem with that is that horrible things can be justified with CO_2 arguments, or tolerated because they have little obvious impact on CO_2. This ersatz "green" argument has been applied to fracking, nuclear power, big hydro, GMOs, and the conversion of forests into wood chips for biofuel. Now you might say these are specious arguments that depend on faulty carbon accounting (is nuclear power really that carbon friendly when you account for the immense amount of energy needed to mine the uranium, refine the uranium, procure the cement, contain the waste, etc.?), but I am afraid there is a deeper problem.

It is that when we base policy on a global metric, *i.e.,* by the numbers, then the numbers are always subject to manipulation by those with the power to do so. Data can be manipulated, factors can be ignored, and projections can be skewed toward optimistic best-case scenarios. This is an inherent problem with basing policy on a metric like tons of CO_2 or GGEs (greenhouse gas equivalents).

Secondly, by focusing on a measurable quantity we devalue that which we cannot measure or choose not to measure. Such issues such as mining, biodiversity, toxic pollution, ecosystem disruption, etc., recede in urgency, because after all, unlike global levels of CO_2 they do not pose an existential threat. Certainly one can make carbon-based arguments on all these issues, but to do so is to step onto dangerous ground.

Imagine that you are trying to stop a strip mine by citing the fuel use of the equipment and the lost carbon sink of the forest that needs to be cleared, and the mining company says, "OK, we're going to do this in the most green way possible; we are going to fuel our bulldozers with biofuels, run our computers on solar power, and plant two trees for every tree we chop down." You get into a tangle of arithmetic, none of which touches the real reason you want to stop the mine - because you love that mountaintop, that forest, those waters that would be poisoned.

I am certain we will not "save our planet" (or at least the ecological basis of civilization) by merely being cleverer in our deployment of Earth's "resources." We will not escape this crisis so long as we see the planet and everything on it as instruments of our utility. The present climate change narrative veers too close to instrumental utilitarian logic - that we should value the earth because of what will happen to us if we don't. Where did we develop the habit of making choices based on maximizing or minimizing a number? We got it from the money world. We are seeking to apply our numbers games to a new target, CO_2 rather than dollars. I don't think that is a deep enough revolution. We need a revolution in means, not only a revolution in ends.

In other words, what we need is a revolution of love. When we as a society learn to see the planet and everything on it as beings deserving of respect - in their own right and not just for their use to us - then we won't need to appeal to climate change to do all the best things that the climate change warriors would have us do. And, we will stop doing the awful things that we do in the name of stopping climate change.

Ironically, many of the environmental issues that seem unrelated to climate change, we are learning, actually do contribute to it. Take hydroelectric dams: they flood forests and wetlands, displace communities, and disrupt riverine ecosystems. But at least they provide climate-friendly electricity, right? Well, no. It turns out that dams and artificial reservoirs emit huge amounts of methane from the rotting vegetation that they generate, and reduce rivers' ability to capture carbon.

Finally, let us admit that our knowledge of Earth's climate homeostasis is quite rudimentary. While we assume that, say, digging gold out of a mountain has little effect on climate, other cultures disagree. A Brazilian friend of mine who works with indigenous tribes there reports that according to them, mining is a much bigger threat to the planet than CO_2, because when metals are removed from the tropics and moved to the temperate zones, the planet's energetics are disrupted. Even taking gold away from a sacred mountain can have devastating effects. A Zuni man I met told me that they believe that the worst thing is to take so much water that the rivers no longer reach the sea - because how then can the ocean know what the land needs?

Let us not be too quick to dismiss such ideas as superstitious fantasy. Time and again, indigenous people have proven that their "superstitions" encode a sophisticated understanding of ecology. While such ideas as "insulting the water" and "stealing the golden soul of the mountains" seem baldly unscientific, we may need to start taking them seriously.

I will end with a prediction. I predict that we will succeed in drastically reducing fossil fuel use, beyond the most optimistic projections - and that climate change will continue to worsen. It might be warming, it might be cooling, it might be intensifying fluctuations, a derangement of normal, life-giving rhythms. Then will we realize the importance of those things that we'd relegated to low priority: the mangrove swamps, the deep aquifers, the sacred sites, the biodiversity hotspots, the virgin forests, the elephants, the whales... all the beings that, in mysterious ways invisible to our numbers, maintain the balance of our living planet. Then will we realize that as we do to any part of nature, so, inescapably, we do to ourselves. The current climate change narrative is but a first step toward that understanding.

I don't in any way disagree with Eisenstein's analysis, but I temper my idealism with a political pragmatism borne of nearly 69 years' experience in the real world. I can show you the scars.

That pragmatic view places me in odd company with President Obama, whom I have frequently criticized and called a war criminal and international scofflaw. In his *Rolling Stone* interview in September, Obama said:

> But if we're going to get our arms around this problem, which I think we can, then we are going to have to take into account the fact that the average American right now, even if they've gotten past climate denial, is still much more concerned about gas prices, getting back and forth from work, than they are about the climate changing. And if we are not strategic about how we talk about the issue and work with all the various stakeholders on this issue, then what will happen is that this will be demagogued and we will find ourselves in a place where we actually have slower progress rather than faster progress.
>
> So the science doesn't change. The urgency doesn't change. But part of my job is to figure out what's my fastest way to get from point A to point B - what's the best way for us to get to a point where we've got a clean-energy economy. And somebody who is not involved in politics may say, "Well, the shortest line between two points is just a straight

line; let's just go straight to it." Well, unfortunately, in a democracy, I may have to zig and zag occasionally, and take into account very real concerns and interests.

I think one of the failures that we had in the cap-and-trade legislation that came up early in my first term was we were doing so many things at that time. People's minds were overwhelmingly focused on economic recovery and getting people back to work - and rightly so - that for a member of Congress who might care about climate change, but was seeing massive job loss, and comes from an industrial state where the [cost of] transition is going to be really high to go from dirty energy to clean energy - casting a vote like that just didn't seem to be a priority. And we hadn't built enough of the consensus that was required to get that done.

***

This is similar to the discussions I have with progressives sometimes when they say, "Why didn't you have a trillion-dollar stimulus instead of an $800 billion stimulus?" And you try to explain, well, this was significantly larger than the New Deal; it was the largest stimulus ever, but I had to get the votes of a couple of Republicans in order to get it done. Or folks who want single-payer health care instead of Obamacare. We had political constraints.

Now, what this tells us, generally, is that those who, rightly, see this as the issue of our time have to take politics into account and have to be strategic in terms of how we frame the issues, and we have to make sure that we're bringing the public along with us. There's been good work done in terms of public education over the last several years. I think surveys show that the American people understand this is an urgent problem. But it isn't yet at the point where they consider it the most important problem, and it's not even close.

The middle path, it seems to me, lies between Eisenstein and Obama. Yes, we should endeavor to bring the public along, but we need to remember what cultural anthropologist Margaret Mead said:

> Never doubt that a small group of thoughtful committed citizens can change the world; indeed, it's the only thing that ever has.

We can be pushing the front edges of what is possible even as we bring up those at the rear. In our work in permaculture and ecovillage-based solutions, we can, through thoughtful design, protect indigenous culture, sacred forests, and biodiversity even as we sequence cascades of food, fiber, medicines, energy, building materials, and diverse ecological services, in sensitive ways that will, in the not-distant future, redefine how humans inhabit their one small planet, the only one we've got.

Realpolitik in Paris

"The question of feasibility is a completely different thing."

"No one wants a repeat of Copenhagen... perhaps the planets were not aligned, but now they are," Laurent Fabius said, as he opened the not-quite final plenary at noon Saturday.

> To conclude, one of us the other day reminded us of Nelson Mandela's sentence: "It always seems impossible until it's done." I wish to add some other words to that, words spoken by the same hero: "None of us acting alone can be successful. Success is built collectively." In this room you are going to be deciding upon a historic agreement. The world is holding its breath. It's counting on all of us."

No one does superlatives better than the French. A blogger for *New Scientist* tweeted: Hollande: "You are on the last step and you must hoist yourself one step higher still."

There are two major competing narratives and a number of minor ones as COP-21 winds down towards its conclusion. Most narratives have it that too much is at stake for the conference to fail and everyone to go home empty-handed - again. And yet that is precisely where the COP was headed as of now, Saturday, awaiting the release of the so-called "final" draft.

Henry Kissinger once famously opined that nations do not behave as individuals do and so one should never negotiate as if they did. Nations are not guided by morality the way people are, but by a calculation of the imperatives of power.

Interests of nations are best served not by striving to dominate or game the system but by recognition of rules and limits among a sophisticated international community that may include actors other than states, such as corporations, activists, and labor unions.

The Clinton-Obama Copenhagen gambit was an effort to break the 15-year logjam over the climate issue by radically restructuring the game being played at the United Nations, from one of sanction-backed mandates (Kyoto) in which bad actors are punished by economic penalties, to one of voluntary pledges in which bad actors are shamed. Under this theory, nations behave as individuals would, seeking praise and avoiding blame. It hasn't worked. Many countries have shown they are shameless. Nonetheless, both India and Saudi Arabia hired high-end PR firms to keep their images up.

Independent analyses of the national pledges, or INDCs, suggest they could put the world on track to warming of between 2.7 and 3.5 °C by 2100, depending on what assumptions are made about emissions after 2030 and ignoring the full system equilibrium calculation which would at least double that temperature range.

"I think it is clear that the INDCs will fall well short of what is required for any reasonable probability of avoiding 2°C," says Alice Bows-Larkin of the Tyndall Centre for Climate Change Research in Manchester, UK. And what happens after 2030 is crucial, too. "We can't assume that emissions will immediately decline."

At a meeting in London on October 28, *New Scientist* asked UNFCCC Chief Christiana Figueres if it was now time for the world to accept that limiting warming to 2°C is unrealistic and to start preparing for even greater warming. Figueres vehemently rejected this idea.

"Would you want that for your children?" she responded. "This is about the quality of life on this planet." The Paris treaty would "build a pathway" to 2°C, she said, by paving the way for further cuts.

Listening for a moment to Henry Kissinger, what is needed is not a praise and blame game but an agreed set of rules. The tough part is reaching agreement on what those rules need to be.

John Schellnhuber of Potsdam Institute for Climate Impact Research, who advises Germany and the Vatican on climate change, says there is a scientific rationale for 1.5C being in the current Paris draft text:

> I have been involved from the very beginning in the 2C target. It was sort of a surprise that the 1.5C came out here so strong in the text. Let's face it, we are still a night away from the final treaty. But we can be pretty sure the 1.5C will be referred to clearly, like we are going to land planet Earth somewhere between 1.5C and 2C, hopefully very close to 1.5C.

> There is a scientific rationale for that. When I have looked into tipping points of the climate system, you discover the real dangers start around 1.5C, 2C. We cannot provide you with that precision. We cannot say Greenland melts at 1.7C and then it's irreversible, but we can say we are entering the risk zone at 1.5C. That is same for the coral reefs.

> In order to be on the safe side it is very wise to consider 1.5C as the right guardrail, given all the uncertainties from risk analyses.

The question of feasibility is a completely different thing.

What I feel is insufficient in the current treaty is that if you say 1.5C then you need [to be] phasing out CO_2 by the middle of this century. You need zero carbon emissions by 2050. If that would also appear in the text than I would be more than happy, and entitled to open a bottle of champagne at Champs Élysées.

There are those who would keep the stopper in Professor Schellnhuber's bottle.

As I reported previously, John Kerry at his Thursday press conference revealed the existence of a shadow "High Ambition Coalition" that had been meeting in secret for 6 months to set high goals for the Paris Agreement. After that revelation, several key players who were not part of the Coalition caucused among their delegations and joined, including Canada, Australia, Brazil, the EU, and the Philippines. The Coalition is chaired by the Marshall Islands, which represents the Island nations, AOSIS, the most vulnerable of all to sea level rise.

Marshall Islands Foreign Minister Tony de Brum revealed to Andrew Freeman of the Associated Press that "Last night we sat in a negotiating room listening to a coordinated campaign to gut the text of ambition":

These included interventions requesting the deletion of long-term emissions pathways, concrete language to land the 5-year revisiting of targets, and a refusal to recognize the science.

According to others in the room, the nations de Brum was referring to were Saudi Arabia, Venezuela, and Russia, with the support of China, India, and Malaysia. These countries sought to remove any references to a global warming target of 1.5 degrees, as well as provisions calling for a mandatory review of countries' emissions reduction plans and full transparency.

He did not name them. That would be shaming. Instead, he merely held out for a firm regulatory context.

"We're not here to accept a minimalist Paris agreement, this is our red line," de Brum said.

Thursday evening's draft agreement aimed for "carbon neutrality" toward the latter half of the century, without defining what that term means. Saturday's draft is expected to instead say "greenhouse gas emissions neutrality," which is more precise and would necessitate a near-complete decarbonization of the world economy by 2100. The High Ambition Coalition was seeking neutrality by 2050. We await the "final" text to clarify this point.

Is that so difficult? Earlier this year Hawaii passed legislation requiring that, by 2045, the entire island will be powered by renewable energy sources. Sweden is on track to be all renewable by 2050. It is more than 60% of the way there. Norway, with its strong hydropower asset, is 98% renewable in the electric sector. Brazil, using ethanol from sugar cane in regenerative, soil-building rotations, is 75% renewable. Denmark, Portugal, Colombia, Venezuela, and Canada produce more than 50% of their electricity from renewables. The United States, after half a century of doing everything it possibly could to torpedo renewables while boosting nuclear and fossil research and development, finds itself at the back in the pack with Australia, Japan, and Poland, at around 12 percent, well below China,

Mexico, India, and Russia, among others. It will have a long way to go if it wants to catch up now.

Richard Heinberg, in *Renewable Energy After COP21: Nine issues for climate leaders to think about on the journey home,* points to more unsuspected hazards in the road to solar:

> While with Level One we began a shift in food systems by promoting local organic food, driving carbon emissions down further will require finishing that job by making all food production organic, and requiring all agriculture to sequester carbon through building topsoil. Eliminating all fossil fuels in food systems will also entail a substantial re-design of those systems to minimize processing, packaging, and transport.
>
> The communications sector - which uses mining and high heat processes for the production of phones, computers, servers, wires, photo-optic cables, cell towers, and more - presents some really knotty problems. The only good long-term solution in this sector is to make devices that are built to last a very long time and then to repair them and fully recycle and re-manufacture them when absolutely needed. The Internet could be maintained via the kinds of low-tech, asynchronous networks now being pioneered in poor nations, using relatively little power.
>
> Back in the transport sector: we've already made shipping more efficient with sails in Level Two, but doing away with petroleum altogether will require costly substitutes (fuel cells or biofuels). One way or another, global trade will have to shrink. There is no good drop-in substitute for aviation fuels; we may have to write off aviation as anything but a specialty transport mode. Planes running on hydrogen or biofuels are an expensive possibility, as are dirigibles filled with (non-renewable) helium, any of which

could help us maintain vestiges of air travel. Paving and repairing roads without oil-based asphalt is possible, but will require an almost complete redesign of processes and equipment.

The good news is that if we do all these things, we can get to beyond zero carbon emissions; that is, with sequestration of carbon in soils and forests, we could actually reduce atmospheric carbon with each passing year.

Ironically, one of the things that could speed up decarbonization is the low price of oil. Anything below $75 per barrel makes extracting from unconventional sources uneconomic. That prevents production, which curtails consumption. To keep the price down, what is needed is not more production - that would be impossible at lower prices - but lower demand, something that is virtually assured in the era of steep contraction that lies ahead, for reasons that have nothing to do with climate change and a lot to do with financial debt overreach.

There is really only one path to salvation, if salvation can be salvaged at this late date. It runs not top-down but bottom-up, through the mass actions of seven billion people. As Charlotte Du Cann, editor of the *Transition Free Press,* wrote:

In the COP21 deal there are blue sky pledges but no mention of how carbon reduction might be achieved on the ground in a world where everything we consume is made possible by oil. The obvious 'solution' to power-down our whole way of life was never on the table. At the COP21 'fringe' however it's clear we need to do exactly that, and undergo what some call *decroissance* (degrowth). To walk in the opposite direction of Empire.

This story is made up of humble things: of cargo bikes and community orchards, of handmade bread and local assemblies, big picture vision, small everyday actions, a tale of sharing and restoration and sincerity and many other things besides. It doesn't fit into a hash tag. It takes time to listen to. It challenges all the assumptions we were taught by our parents and teachers, and most avowedly, by our governments.

The meeting adjourns until 3:45 pm to allow text to be first translated, then distributed, then read. Time for all to go for a long French déjeuner. Back later, after we are joined by our West Coast affiliates....

Saturday Night, December 12, 2015

Here Comes The Sun

"The COP agreed that the era of fossil energy is over. That is no longer in question. It will end by 2050, if not sooner. The question is how, and the Paris Agreement leaves that to fairy dust."

At 7:27 pm Paris time (ECT), the President of the COP, French Foreign Minister Laurent Fabius, gavelled the Paris Agreement home. The crowd stood, applauded, and whooped. The text is provided in an appendix at the end of this book.

Success, it seemed to us, came because of the unions. They were not dockworkers or ironmongers. They were unions of countries with brands that read like corporate logos: AOSIS, AILAC, ALBA, G77 Plus, High Ambition, the Like-Minded. No single effort could broker a deal unless it got the big unions on board. In the end ALBA (Alliance for the Peoples of our America - Venezuela, Bolivia, Nicaragua, Ecuador and Cuba) and stealth-OPEC (Arab States) were too small to matter. The Like-Minded splintered in favor of the Ambitious. The Climate Vulnerable Forum and High Ambition ruled.

In their 2-minute closer, the Philippines noted it was the first time that the concept of climate justice appears in a legally binding document. In time, they hinted, the United States and other overdeveloped countries will be made to pay reparations to those who will lose all or substantial parts of their countries, including all that high-priced real estate in Rio, Guangzhou, Mumbai, and Shanghai. Consumerist Empires built on fossil energy may have an unusually large credit card statement coming at the end of the billing cycle. Philippines Climate Change Commissioner Emmanuel "Manny" De Guzman said:

> The Paris Agreement is a significant stride forward for several reasons:
>
> First, its 1.5°C goal has defined the global ambition for climate action. Paris has given us 1.5°C to survive and to thrive. We've seen how Parties coalesced around this goal. And we shall deliver on this goal. The Climate Vulnerability Forum, led by the Philippines, will continue to lead and sustain the fight against climate change for a safe and resilient future for all.
>
> Second, the Agreement enshrines human rights as its bedrock principle, including the rights of indigenous peoples, women, and migrants, among others. Although we would have preferred stronger language on human rights, in adopting the Paris Agreement, the era of climate justice has come. We are very pleased that for the first time, we have enshrined climate justice in an international legally binding agreement.
>
> Third, the Agreement ensures ecosystem integrity in climate actions, an element that we are also pleased with.
>
> Fourth, the Agreement ensures support in finance, technology, and capacity building for all adaptation and mitigation efforts. While we are already doing a lot on our own to adapt to and mitigate climate change, we are committed to do much more as our INDC shows, and we can do more with the support of our partners.
>
> We would have wanted quantitative targets and more legally binding language and we will continue to work for these as we implement the agreement.

Lastly, we joined other developing countries in fighting for the inclusion of a Loss and Damage Article in the Agreement, separate from Adaptation, to secure the permanence of the Warsaw International Mechanism on Loss and Damage.

It lays the foundation for what we like to refer to as the WIM Plus: an institutionalized, operationalized Mechanism on Loss and Damage that would ensure the recovery, restoration, and resilience of communities, livelihoods and ecosystems adversely affected by slow onset events, extreme weather events, and other climate change impacts. We are concerned with paragraph 52 of the decision. We will study its long-term implications and will engage with partners on this at a later stage.

Our Paris Agreement may not be as perfect as we want it to be, but it is essentially an acceptable accord. We can build on it and make it better over time. We must now focus on its implementation and on the compliance procedures and will engage in the process.

Pluses and minuses in the new agreement: the 1.5C target is in, thanks to the efforts of UNFCCC head Christina Figueres to give a voice to civil society in these corridors. Five-year "stocktakes" (Webster's Dictionary please take note) - reassessment of progress and commitments - are in. Full phase-out of fossil energy by 2050 is not, but that door is not entirely closed and may be reopened at Marrakech next year.

Each Party's successive nationally determined contribution will represent a progression beyond the Party's then current nationally determined contribution and reflect its highest possible ambition, reflecting its common but differentiated responsibilities and respective capabilities, in the light of different national circumstances.

What the text mandates, which is actually significant, is to "achieve a balance between anthropogenic emissions by sources and removals by sinks of greenhouse gases in the second half of this century, on the basis of equity, and in the context of sustainable development and efforts to eradicate poverty."

Decarbonization by 2050 is no longer just a t-shirt. Now it's international law.

Bill McKibben said:

> Every government seems now to recognize that the fossil fuel era must end and soon. But the power of the fossil fuel industry is reflected in the text, which drags out the transition so far that endless climate damage will be done. Since pace is the crucial question now, activists must redouble our efforts to weaken that industry. This didn't save the planet but it may have saved the chance of saving the planet.

350.org Executive director, May Boeve, said:

> This marks the end of the era of fossil fuels. There is no way to meet the targets laid out in this agreement without keeping coal, oil and gas in the ground. The text should send a clear signal to fossil fuel investors: divest now.

> The final text still has some serious gaps. We're very concerned about the exclusion of the rights of indigenous peoples, the lack of finance for loss and damage, and that while the text recognizes the importance of keeping global warming below 1.5 degrees C, the current commitments from countries still add up to well over 3 degrees of warming. These are red lines we cannot cross. After Paris,

we'll be redoubling our efforts to deliver the real solutions that science and justice demand.

The think-tank E3G said, "The transition to a low carbon economy is now unstoppable, ensuring the end of the fossil fuel age."

Carbon Tracker said, "Fossil fuel companies will need to accept that they are ex-growth stocks and must urgently reassess their business plans accordingly."

The Guardian called it a "victory for climate science and ultimate defeat for fossil fuels."

Rolling Stone reporter Jeff Goodell wrote:

> As far as the details of the Paris agreement go, there are two big accomplishments worth mentioning. The first is that it more or less eliminated the old distinction between developed and developing countries, which was enshrined in the 1997 Kyoto Protocol and led to two decades of political warfare both in the U.S. and abroad (and was one of the big reasons the Kyoto Protocol was never ratified by the U.S.). The basic idea was that the developed world - i.e., the U.S. and the European Union - bore the burden for cutting emissions first, largely because they were the ones who had caused the problem with their 150-year-long fossil fuel party. In order to grow, the developing world - i.e. China and India - believed it had the right to do the same thing. This binary distinction was a big diplomatic blunder, not only because developing nations like China and India are quickly becoming the largest carbon polluters on the planet (even if per capita emissions are well below the U.S.), but also because it created a political dynamic in the U.S. that allowed deniers in Congress to argue that if China and India weren't doing anything to solve the problem, why should we? The Paris agreement eliminates

the old binary distinction - now nations are expected to contribute to the best of their abilities. By putting everyone in the same boat, the Paris agreement underscores an essential truth: We have one atmosphere, and if we screw it up, everyone suffers.

The second big accomplishment is that the agreement sets up a kind of public accounting method for carbon pollution (and one which, unlike commitments to emissions reductions, will be legally binding). Public accounting is key to making sure the emissions reductions that nations claim they are making are real, and not just carbon PR designed to boost their status as good global citizens. Accounting standards will take time to evolve, but the Paris agreement at least begins the process.

One piece of statecraft managed by Obama and Kerry was to neatly skirt what killed Kyoto: the 60 Neanderthals in the US Senate put there by the coal kings. *The New York Times* spotted the play and reported:

Some elements of the accord would be voluntary, while others would be legally binding. That hybrid structure was specifically intended to ensure the support of the United States: An accord that would have required legally binding targets for emissions reductions would be legally interpreted as a new treaty, and would be required to go before the Senate for ratification.

Such a proposal would be dead on arrival in the Republican-controlled Senate, where many lawmakers question the established science of climate change, and where even more hope to thwart President Obama's climate change agenda.

***

The accord uses the language of an existing treaty, the 1992 United Nations Framework Convention on Climate Change, to put forth legally binding language requiring countries to verify their emissions, and to periodically put forth new, tougher domestic plans over time.

In just updating regulations enacted under an already ratified treaty, the Paris Agreement bypasses the need for new Senate ratification.

Inside Le Bourget, after the obligatory high-fives and selfies, delegates crafted sound bites for the press and kept the lights on and microphones active past midnight. Outside, 10,000 activists took to the streets to pull a "red line," representing 1.5 degrees, to the Arc de Triomphe.

The Day After

We are a lucky species in that our optimism is more or less hard-wired.

The speeches went on at Le Bourget until after midnight, but most of the delegates had already found their ways to receptions where champagne was uncorked and laughter and gaiety filled the night.

French President Francois Hollande, who has a gift for hyperbole, said, "History is made by those who commit, not those who calculate. Today you committed. You did not calculate." Although not in the way he meant it, this is ironically a first-rate assessment of the Agreement.

There is a quality of awareness among all the delegates to the Paris climate talks that, after 20 years of these discussions, is passing strange. We would not call it a deer-in-the-headlights look, because it is not even quite there yet. Those jockeying for the best outcome for their own economies and constituencies are still quite oblivious to the science of what is transpiring and the dire nature of the threat. They have their noses down in the trough and do not hear the butcher at the barn door.

This should not be surprising. Nowhere in the fossil record is there anything quite like what is transforming the world of humans today. Our physical brains are virtually the same as they were 30,000 years ago, when we were standing upright in the savannah, alert to proximate, not distant, threats and quickly obtained, not slowly exploited, resources.

We make ourselves ignorant in at least three ways: not knowing the basic science of climate change, not knowing what to do about it once we become aware of the problem, and being barraged with wrong information about both of those and being unable to distinguish fact from fiction.

We might think that a lamb raised in New Zealand and eaten in London would create more greenhouse gases than one being locally grown, but in the way the world works today, the opposite is true. We might think that going vegan is more climate-responsible than raising farmed animals, but because of how pastured animals stock soils with carbon, the opposite can be true. We might think, as climate scientist James Hansen does, that low prices for gas cause more fossil fuels to be burned, but the opposite is true, because low prices keep whole provinces of production from being tapped.

When disciplined and deliberate attempts by profit-driven vested interests in the production of greenhouse gases cast doubt on science, and corrupt politics and the media, grasping these nuances becomes even more difficult.

We are a lucky species in that our optimism is more or less hard-wired. People tend to be overly optimistic about their chances of having a happy marriage or avoiding illness. Young people are easily lured to join the military, become combat photographers or medics, or engage in extreme-risk sports because they are unrealistically optimistic they can avoid harm. Humans are also overly optimistic about environmental risks. Our confirmation bias helps us keep up this optimism even when confronted with scientific truths to the contrary.

The principal outcome is less about the *how* than about the *whether*. The COP agreed that the era of fossil energy is over. That is no longer in question. It will end by 2050, if not sooner. The question is how, and the Paris Agreement leaves that to fairy dust.

The Guardian reported:

> Throughout the week, campaigners have said the deal had to send a clear signal to global industry that the era of fossil fuels was ending. Scientists have seen the moment as career defining.

Carbon Tracker said:

> New energy technologies have become hugely cost-competitive in recent years and the effect of the momentum created in Paris will only accelerate that trend. The need for financial markets to fund the clean energy transition creates opportunity for growth on a scale not seen since the industrial revolution.

What will replace fossil energy? The basket of renewables described by Jeremy Leggett in *The Winning of the Carbon War*? There is a slight problem there, and one wonders how long it will take for that to catch up to the delegates. Perhaps by the first stocktake, but maybe longer.

Richard Heinberg, Senior Fellow at the Post-Carbon Institute writes in *Renewable Energy After COP21: Nine issues for climate leaders to think about on the journey home*:

> The fact that the fossil fuel industry will require ever-increasing levels of investment per unit of energy yielded has a gloomy implication for the energy transition:

society's available capital will have to be directed toward the deteriorating fossil fuel sector to maintain current services, just as much more capital is also needed to fund the build-out of renewables. Seemingly the only way to avoid this trap would be to push the energy transition as quickly as possible, so that we aren't stuck two or three decades from now still dependent on fossil fuels that, by then, will be requiring so much investment to find and extract that society may not be able to afford the transition project.

But there's also a problem with accelerating the transition too much. Since we use fossil fuels to build the infrastructure for renewables, speeding up the transition could mean an overall increase in emissions - unless we reduce other current uses of fossil fuels. In other words, we may have to deprive some sectors of the economy of fossil fuels before adequate renewable substitutes are available, in order to fuel the transition without increasing overall greenhouse gas emissions. This would translate to a reduction in overall energy consumption and in the economic benefits of energy use (though money saved from conservation and efficiency would hopefully reduce the impact), and this would have to be done without producing a regressive impact on already vulnerable and economically disadvantaged communities.

The elephant in the room, as elaborated in our book, the *Post-Petroleum Survival Guide* (2006), is net energy, or return on energy investment (EROEI), first delineated by systems ecologist Howard T. Odum. These days the leading scientists in that field are calling it "biophysical economics."

When the EROEI of a resource is less than or equal to one, that energy source becomes a net "energy sink," and can no longer be used as a source of energy, but depending on the system might be useful for energy storage (for example a battery, or the tidal storage in Scotland). The source of almost all our energy is the sun but a fuel or energy source must have an EROEI ratio of at least 3:1 to be considered viable. This chart shows typical values for various technologies.

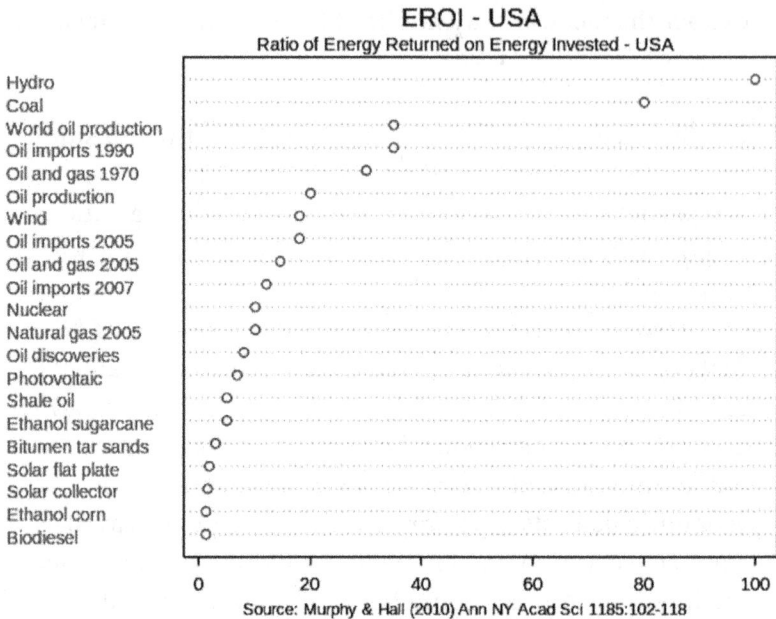

EROI - USA
Ratio of Energy Returned on Energy Invested - USA

Hydro	~90
Coal	~75
World oil production	~30
Oil imports 1990	~30
Oil and gas 1970	~25
Oil production	~18
Wind	~16
Oil imports 2005	~16
Oil and gas 2005	~13
Oil imports 2007	~12
Nuclear	~10
Natural gas 2005	~10
Oil discoveries	~8
Photovoltaic	~7
Shale oil	~5
Ethanol sugarcane	~5
Bitumen tar sands	~4
Solar flat plate	~3
Solar collector	~2
Ethanol corn	~2
Biodiesel	~2

Source: Murphy & Hall (2010) Ann NY Acad Sci 1185:102-118

Right now most of what powers the world comes from the top half of that chart. The Paris agreement suggests that most of what we need by 2050 must be selected from portions of the bottom half of the chart - the so-called "clean" energies." Quoth the prophet, Wikipedia:

> Thomas Homer-Dixon argues that a falling EROEI in the Later Roman Empire was one of the reasons for the collapse of the Western Empire in the fifth century CE. In *"The Upside of Down"* he suggests that EROEI analysis provides a basis for the analysis of the rise and fall of

civilizations. Looking at the maximum extent of the Roman Empire (60 million), and its technological base, the agrarian base of Rome was about 1:12 per hectare for wheat and 1:27 for alfalfa (giving a 1:2.7 production for oxen). One can then use this to calculate the population of the Roman Empire required at its height, on the basis of about 2,500-3,000 calories per day per person. It comes out roughly equal to the area of food production at its height. But ecological damage (deforestation, soil fertility loss particularly in southern Spain, southern Italy, Sicily and especially north Africa) saw a collapse in the system beginning in the 2nd century, as EROEI began to fall. It bottomed in 1084 when Rome's population, which had peaked under Trajan at 1.5 million, was only 15,000. Evidence also fits the cycle of Mayan and Cambodian collapse too. Joseph Tainter suggests that diminishing returns of the EROEI is a chief cause of the collapse of complex societies; this has been suggested as caused by peak wood in early societies. Falling EROEI due to depletion of high quality fossil fuel resources also poses a difficult challenge for industrial economies.

When we hear pleas from underdeveloping countries for greater financial assistance to allow them to adapt - meaning building out renewable energy and migrating coastal cities inland - we have to ask ourselves if they really comprehend what they will need to adapt to, and whether any amount of money will ever be enough. The *status quo ante* - the way things worked before - is gone, and so is the *modo omnia futura*. One hundred billion dollars per year is not enough to save human beings as a species, but asking for more won't help, either. What might help is committing to degrowth, to depopulation, and to scaling back our human footprint to something closer to what we had coming out of the last Ice Age, before we started building monumental cities, mining metal, and inventing writing.

We don't need to abandon writing, but let's get real - those megacities may be unsalvageable on a solar budget.

Richard Heinberg points to a few more elephants, standing in the corridor and waiting to get into the room:

> We may be entering a period of fossil fuel triage. Rather than allocating fossil fuels simply on a market basis (those who pay for them get them), it may be fairer, especially to lower-income citizens, for government (with wartime powers) to allocate fuels purposefully based on the strategic importance of the societal sectors that depend on them, and on the relative ease and timeliness of transitioning those sectors to renewable substitutes. Agriculture, for example, might be deemed the highest priority for continued fossil fuel allocations, with commercial air travel assuming a far lower priority. Perhaps we need not just a price on carbon, but different prices for different uses. We see very little discussion of this prospect in the current energy policy literature. Further, few governments even currently acknowledge the need for a carbon budget. The political center of gravity, particularly in the United States, will have to shift significantly before decision-makers can publicly acknowledge the need for fossil fuel triage.
>
> As fossil fuels grow more costly to extract, there may be ever-greater temptation to use our available energy and investment capital merely to maintain existing consumption patterns (likely for the rich above all), and to put off the effort that the transition implies. If we do that, we will eventually reap the worst of all possible outcomes - climate chaos, a gutted economy, and no continuing wherewithal to build a bridge to a renewable energy future.

Studies claiming that a transition to renewable energy will be easy and cost-free may allay fears and thus help speed the transition. However, sweeping actual difficulties under the carpet also delays confronting them. We need to start now to address the problems of energy demand adaptation, of balancing intermittency in energy supply from solar and wind, and of energy substitution in thousands of industrial processes. Those are big jobs, and ignoring them won't make them go away.

Kumi Naidoo of Greenpeace said, "We have a 1.5C wall to climb but the ladder is not tall enough." But he acknowledged, "As a result of what we have secured here we will win... for us Paris was always a stop on an ongoing journey... I believe we are now in with a serious chance to succeed."

Glen Peters, scientist at CICERO[95], said 1.5C effectively requires a fossil fuel phase-out by 2030. He later clarified that was without negative emissions or the immediate introduction of a global carbon price, which are some of the assumptions in 1.5C models. His personal view was chances of achieving 1.5C were "extremely slim."

Will voluntary pledges, revisited every five years starting in 2023, be enough to cut emissions and hold to the budget? It is the wrong question. That budget does not exist. Closer scrutiny of embedded systemic feedbacks reveal we'd blown though any possible atmospheric buffer zone by the 1970s and have just been piling on carbon up there every since.

---

[95] Center for International Climate and Environmental Research - Oslo

The Atlantic reported:

> Recent science has indicated that warming to two degrees, still the stated international red line, might be catastrophic, creating mega-hurricanes and possibly halting the temperate jet stream which waters American and European farmland.
>
> From that perspective, 1.5 degrees is an encouraging, ambitious goal. But it's also a promise that costs negotiators nothing while indicating great moral seriousness.
>
> Because here's the thing: The math still doesn't work. 2015 is the hottest year on measure. Because of the delay between when carbon enters the atmosphere and when it traps heat, we are nearly locked into nearly 1.5 degrees of warming already. Many thought the world would abandon the two-degree target at Paris due to its impracticality.

Once we apply honestly science-based Earth system sensitivity at equilibrium, excluding none of the feedbacks and forcings that we know of, we discover we passed the 2°C target in 1978. To hold at 2 degrees we would need to bring CO_2 concentration down to 334 ppm, not increase it to 450 or 500 as the Paris Agreement contemplates. To hold at 1.5°C we would need to vacuum the atmosphere even lower, to a level last seen some time before mid-20th century.

Outside of elite scientists such as those we've mentioned or run into this past week - Anderson, Schellnhuber, Rockstrom,[96] Hansen, Wasdell, and Goreau - few in Le Bourget seem to grasp some simple arithmetic. And so we

---

[96] Johan Rockström is vice-chair of the Scientific Advisory Board of the Potsdam Institute for Climate Impact Research and chair of the Earth System Visioning Task Team.

are treated to the spectacle of fossil producers like India, Russia, Saudi Arabia, and many other countries demanding more time to fill up the available atmospheric space, when in reality there is none and hasn't been for quite some time.

In his September interview with *Rolling Stone*, President Obama said:

> I'm less concerned about the precise number, because let's stipulate right now, whatever various country targets are, it's still going to fall short of what the science requires. So a percent here or a percent there coming from various countries is not going to be a deal-breaker. But making sure everybody is making serious efforts and that we are making a joint international commitment that is well-defined and can be measured will create the basis for us each year, then, to evaluate, "How are we doing?" and will allow us, five years from now, to say the science is new, we need to ratchet it up, and by the way, because of the research and development that we've put in, we can achieve more ambitious goals.
>
> And the key for Paris is just to make sure that everybody is locked in, saying, "We're going to do this." Once we get to that point, then we can turn the dials. But there will be a momentum that is built, and I'm confident that we will then be in a position to listen more carefully to the science - partly because people, I think, will be not as fearful of the consequences or as cynical about what can be achieved. Hope builds on itself. Success breeds success.

Some say the UN is hamstrung by multilateral consensus, but voting would be no better. After the COP meeting in Durban, the UNFCCC adopted a traditional South African negotiating format to speed up decision-making and bring opposing countries together. *The Guardian's* John Vidal explains:

> Zulu and Xhosa communities use "indabas" to give everyone equal opportunity to voice their opinions in order to work toward consensus.
>
> They were first used in UN climate talks in Durban in 2011 when, with the talks deadlocked and the summit just minutes from collapse, the South African presidency asked the main countries to form a standing circle in the middle of hundreds of delegates and to talk directly to each other.
>
> Instead of repeating stated positions, diplomats were encouraged to talk personally and quietly about their "red lines" and to propose solutions to each other.
>
> By including everyone and allowing often hostile countries to speak in earshot of observers, it achieved a remarkable breakthrough within 30 minutes.
>
> In Paris the indaba format was used by France to narrow differences between countries behind closed doors. It is said to have rapidly slimmed down a ballooning text with hundreds of potential points of disagreements.
>
> By Wednesday with agreement still far away, French Prime Minister Laurent Fabius further refined the indaba by splitting groups into two.

"It is a very effective way to streamline negotiations and bridge differences. It has the advantage of being participatory yet fair," said one West African diplomat. "It should be used much more when no way through a problem can be found."

What may need to happen next year in Marrakech is that the COP host an indaba with experts both in the climate sciences and in biophysical economics.

As I read through the text looking for places to insert permaculture into the process and put the natural healing processes of the planet to work, I found what may hold the best hope buried 20 pages in, at Article 4:

> In order to achieve the long-term temperature goal set out in Article 2, Parties aim to reach global peaking of greenhouse gas emissions as soon as possible, recognizing that peaking will take longer for developing country Parties, and to undertake rapid reductions thereafter in accordance with best available science, so as to achieve a balance between anthropogenic emissions by sources and removals by sinks of greenhouse gases in the second half of this century, on the basis of equity, and in the context of sustainable development and efforts to eradicate poverty...

and Article 5:

> 1. Parties should take action to conserve and enhance, as appropriate, sinks and reservoirs of greenhouse gases as referred to in Article 4, paragraph 1(d), of the Convention, including forests.

> 2. Parties are encouraged to take action to implement and support, including through results-based payments, the existing framework as set out in related guidance and decisions already agreed under the Convention for: policy approaches and positive incentives for activities relating to reducing emissions from deforestation and forest degradation, and the role of conservation, sustainable management of forests and enhancement of forest carbon stocks in developing countries; and alternative policy approaches, such as joint mitigation and adaptation

approaches for the integral and sustainable management of forests, while reaffirming the importance of incentivizing, as appropriate, non-carbon benefits associated with such approaches.

It is not yet clear whether integrated food- and fuel-sequenced, permaculturally-designed forests - composed of mixed-aged, mixed-species robust ecologies and maximum carbon sequestration though biomass-to-biochar energy, aquaculture and agriculture systems - will be scaled fast enough, but these two articles could be the spark they need to spur investment.

As the clock ticked on towards the new day, the leader of the High Ambition group, Tony de Brum, introduced to the plenary Selina Leem, an 18-year-old from Majuro who spoke of water gradually rising on both sides of her home.

> The coconut leaves I wear in my hair and hold up in my hand is from my home in the Marshall Islands. I wear them today in hope of keeping them for my children and my grandchildren - a symbol, these simple strands of coconut leaves that I hold.... I hope you keep this and show it to your children and grandchildren, and tell them a new story - of how you helped a little island and the whole world today. This agreement is for those of us whose identity, whose culture, whose ancestors, whose whole being, is bound to their lands. I have only spoken about myself and my islands but the same story will play out everywhere in the world.

This conference was not the end of the process. It was a beginning. It was not the end of the challenge to human ingenuity that climate change will pose. It was only the start. Despite the violent street attacks a week before the conference, the knee-jerk police state response, the tepid protests, the suppression of tepid protests, the marginalization of some important stakeholders, the omissions in the text, and the gaps that will have to be bridged at COPs to come, it was an auspicious beginning. The weather stayed mild, the trees continued to drop leaves of yellows and reds, and Paris can be exquisitely charming in December.

Epilogue: The Right Moment

"You want to be a billionaire? Solve a billion-person problem." - Peter Diamandis[97]

We are meeting with government officials of X country. X has a serious dilemma, one which is not uncommon in this era, and which will become the norm for most countries very soon. X is throwing vast sums - 60 billion this year - into finding oil.

It does not consider the dilemma of what happens if it finds the oil and then cannot drill and sell it because to do so would be counterproductive to survival of life on the planet. It does not consider what might happen if it were extraordinarily lucky in its exploration and happened upon such great wealth that it attracted the interest of militarily powerful and ambitious neighbors. It does not consider the potential downside of a boom and bust cycle a favorable discovery of any size would augur, or the destruction of indigenous culture, endangered species, or fragile habitats. It just wants the oil, for its own sake. It is like the truck driver on a long-distance haul across Texas after midnight. It is locked into the white stripe, in the groove, doing whatever comes next, without much thought or planning.

I tell the government officials that I can provide more power than they need, at a tenth of the cost of the oil, and I can do it from feedstocks they consider wastes, and I can use processes that net-sequester greenhouse gases at each

---

[97] Peter Diamandis runs the X Prize Foundation, which offers large cash incentive prizes to inventors who can solve grand challenges like space flight, low-cost mobile medical diagnostics and oil spill cleanup. He is the chair of Singularity University.

step, with a life-cycle cost that is high in the black, low capital outlay, and quick return on investment. Oh, and it arrests global warming, deepens soils, saves water, and increases biodiversity while preserving and protecting indigenous culture.

Naturally, they are incredulous.

Surely we are trying to sell them snake oil, what we propose is illegal, or there is some neglected externality in our calculus that makes our proposal fall apart once exposed to serious scrutiny.

I say, no, actually. We have already vetted all these steps we propose. They follow a simple formula that has no secrets, no privacy, no confidentiality contracts, and anyone could replicate them in whole or part if they so desire. I list our tool kit: biochar, ecovillage design, permaculture, holistic management, keyline water systems, native agroforestry, alley cropping cell divisions, constructed wetlands and chinampas, leaf protein extraction, bioenergy crops that first produce food, and productive, satisfying and fun things for people to be doing together.

I say that if we do this, and others do also, we can stop destructive climate change without worrying about the outcome of the Paris climate talks in December, the obstructionist control of legislators, or the collapse of global Ponzinomic finance. It is justified solely by energy 5 times cheaper than solar cells and better, nutrient-dense food, produced without all the costs of pesticides, herbicides, antibiotics, and fertilizers. It solves so many seemingly intractable problems simultaneously that once set in motion it will never be arrested. It will create a garden planet.

The officials are both nonplussed and unwavering. They use all the standard cop-outs: buck-passing to higher authority, decrying the state of the legal system, urging we wait for a more politically attuned administration and perhaps spend that interim working for its election, and suggesting the need for further study.

No matter, whether the Paris outcome is too little too late; whether the price of oil goes up north of $100 again or south to new lows below $25; whether governments come or governments go. Weather drives this market. The wise will look towards shelter. Once this package is readily available, and the expense is more than justified by immediate returns, the product will sell. Little, short of catastrophic economic collapse, can stop it.

This is an actual conversation I had earlier in 2015, in the run-up to Paris. In Paris, it happened again, only with financial advisors managing billions in assets, and high-net-worth individuals concerned for the future, sitting in gourmet bistros under the Eiffel Tower and on the Seine, in hotel lobbies and in the halls of Le Bourget. There is a change in the wind. Whether it is enough - and we will have time to see it come to fruition - is yet unknown. But the change is real, it is proven, and now, with the Paris Agreement, it begins to accelerate.

> *"Another world is possible. On a clear day I can hear her breathing."*

> - Arundhati Roy

PARIS AGREEMENT

The Parties to this Agreement,

Being Parties to the United Nations Framework Convention on Climate Change, hereinafter referred to as "the Convention",

Pursuant to the Durban Platform for Enhanced Action established by decision 1/CP.17 of the Conference of the Parties to the Convention at its seventeenth session,

In pursuit of the objective of the Convention, and being guided by its principles, including the principle of equity and common but differentiated responsibilities and respective capabilities, in the light of different national circumstances,

Recognizing the need for an effective and progressive response to the urgent threat of climate change on the basis of the best available scientific knowledge,

Also recognizing the specific needs and special circumstances of developing country Parties, especially those that are particularly vulnerable to the adverse effects of climate change, as provided for in the Convention,

Taking full account of the specific needs and special situations of the least developed countries with regard to funding and transfer of technology,

Recognizing that Parties may be affected not only by climate change, but also by the impacts of the measures taken in response to it,

Emphasizing the intrinsic relationship that climate change actions, responses and impacts have with equitable access to sustainable development and eradication of poverty,

Recognizing the fundamental priority of safeguarding food security and ending hunger, and the particular vulnerabilities of food production systems to the adverse impacts of climate change,

Taking into account the imperatives of a just transition of the workforce and the creation of decent work and quality jobs in accordance with nationally defined development priorities,

Acknowledging that climate change is a common concern of humankind, Parties should, when taking action to address climate change, respect, promote and consider their respective obligations on human rights, the right to health, the rights of indigenous peoples, local communities, migrants, children, persons with disabilities and people in vulnerable situations and the right to development, as well as gender equality, empowerment of women and intergenerational equity,

Recognizing the importance of the conservation and enhancement, as appropriate, of sinks and reservoirs of the greenhouse gases referred to in the Convention,

Noting the importance of ensuring the integrity of all ecosystems, including oceans, and the protection of biodiversity, recognized by some cultures as Mother Earth, and noting the importance for some of the concept of "climate justice", when taking action to address climate change,

Affirming the importance of education, training, public awareness, public participation, public access to information and cooperation at all levels on the matters addressed in this Agreement,

Recognizing the importance of the engagements of all levels of government and various actors, in accordance with respective national legislations of Parties, in addressing climate change,

Also recognizing that sustainable lifestyles and sustainable patterns of consumption and production, with developed country Parties taking the lead, play an important role in addressing climate change,

Have agreed as follows:

Article 1

For the purpose of this Agreement, the definitions contained in Article 1 of the Convention shall apply. In addition:

1. "Convention" means the United Nations Framework Convention on Climate Change, adopted in New York on 9 May 1992.

2. "Conference of the Parties" means the Conference of the Parties to the Convention.

3. "Party" means a Party to this Agreement.

Article 2

1. This Agreement, in enhancing the implementation of the Convention, including its objective, aims to strengthen the global response to the threat of climate change, in the context of sustainable development and efforts to eradicate poverty, including by:

(a) Holding the increase in the global average temperature to well below 2 °C above pre-industrial levels and to pursue efforts to limit the temperature increase to 1.5 °C above pre-industrial levels, recognizing that this would significantly reduce the risks and impacts of climate change;

(b) Increasing the ability to adapt to the adverse impacts of climate change and foster climate resilience and low greenhouse gas emissions development, in a manner that does not threaten food production;

(c) Making finance flows consistent with a pathway towards low greenhouse gas emissions and climate-resilient development.

2. This Agreement will be implemented to reflect equity and the principle of common but differentiated responsibilities and respective capabilities, in the light of different national circumstances.

Article 3

As nationally determined contributions to the global response to climate change, all Parties are to undertake and communicate ambitious efforts as defined in Articles 4, 7, 9, 10, 11 and 13 with the view to achieving the purpose of this Agreement as set out in Article 2. The efforts of all Parties will represent a progression over time, while recognizing the need to support developing country Parties for the effective implementation of this Agreement.

Article 4

1. In order to achieve the long-term temperature goal set out in Article 2, Parties aim to reach global peaking of greenhouse gas emissions as soon as possible, recognizing that peaking will take longer for developing country Parties, and to undertake rapid reductions thereafter in accordance with best available science, so as to achieve a balance between anthropogenic emissions by sources and removals by sinks of greenhouse gases in the second half of this century, on the basis of equity, and in the context of sustainable development and efforts to eradicate poverty.

2. Each Party shall prepare, communicate and maintain successive nationally determined contributions that it intends to achieve. Parties shall pursue domestic mitigation measures, with the aim of achieving the objectives of such contributions.

3. Each Party's successive nationally determined contribution will represent a progression beyond the Party's then current nationally determined contribution and reflect its highest possible ambition, reflecting its common but differentiated responsibilities and respective capabilities, in the light of different national circumstances.

4. Developed country Parties should continue taking the lead by undertaking economy-wide absolute emission reduction targets. Developing country Parties should continue enhancing their mitigation efforts, and are encouraged to move over time towards economy-wide emission reduction or limitation targets in the light of different national circumstances.

5. Support shall be provided to developing country Parties for the implementation of this Article, in accordance with Articles 9, 10 and 11, recognizing that enhanced support for developing country Parties will allow for higher ambition in their actions.

6. The least developed countries and small island developing States may prepare and communicate strategies, plans and actions for low greenhouse gas emissions development reflecting their special circumstances.

7. Mitigation co-benefits resulting from Parties' adaptation actions and/or economic diversification plans can contribute to mitigation outcomes under this Article.

8. In communicating their nationally determined contributions, all Parties shall provide the information necessary for clarity, transparency and understanding in accordance with decision 1/CP.21 and any relevant decisions of the Conference of the

Parties serving as the meeting of the Parties to the Paris Agreement.

9. Each Party shall communicate a nationally determined contribution every five years in accordance with decision 1/CP.21 and any relevant decisions of the Conference of the Parties serving as the meeting of the Parties to the Paris Agreement and be informed by the outcomes of the global stocktake referred to in Article 14.

10. The Conference of the Parties serving as the meeting of the Parties to the Paris Agreement shall consider common time frames for nationally determined contributions at its first session.

11. A Party may at any time adjust its existing nationally determined contribution with a view to enhancing its level of ambition, in accordance with guidance adopted by the Conference of the Parties serving as the meeting of the Parties to the Paris Agreement.

12. Nationally determined contributions communicated by Parties shall be recorded in a public registry maintained by the secretariat.

13. Parties shall account for their nationally determined contributions. In accounting for anthropogenic emissions and removals corresponding to their nationally determined contributions, Parties shall promote environmental integrity, transparency, accuracy, completeness, comparability and consistency, and ensure the avoidance of double counting, in accordance with guidance adopted by the Conference of the Parties serving as the meeting of the Parties to the Paris Agreement.

14. In the context of their nationally determined contributions, when recognizing and implementing mitigation actions with

respect to anthropogenic emissions and removals, Parties should take into account, as appropriate, existing methods and guidance under the Convention, in the light of the provisions of paragraph 13 of this Article.

15. Parties shall take into consideration in the implementation of this Agreement the concerns of Parties with economies most affected by the impacts of response measures, particularly developing country Parties.

16. Parties, including regional economic integration organizations and their member States, that have reached an agreement to act jointly under paragraph 2 of this Article shall notify the secretariat of the terms of that agreement, including the emission level allocated to each Party within the relevant time period, when they communicate their nationally determined contributions. The secretariat shall in turn inform the Parties and signatories to the Convention of the terms of that agreement.

17. Each party to such an agreement shall be responsible for its emission level as set out in the agreement referred to in paragraph 16 above in accordance with paragraphs 13 and 14 of this Article and Articles 13 and 15.

18. If Parties acting jointly do so in the framework of, and together with, a regional economic integration organization which is itself a Party to this Agreement, each member State of that regional economic integration organization individually, and together with the regional economic integration organization, shall be responsible for its emission level as set out in the agreement communicated under paragraph 16 of this Article in accordance with paragraphs 13 and 14 of this Article and Articles 13 and 15.

19. All Parties should strive to formulate and communicate long-term low greenhouse gas emission development strategies,

mindful of Article 2 taking into account their common but differentiated responsibilities and respective capabilities, in the light of different national circumstances.

Article 5

1. Parties should take action to conserve and enhance, as appropriate, sinks and reservoirs of greenhouse gases as referred to in Article 4, paragraph 1(d), of the Convention, including forests.

2. Parties are encouraged to take action to implement and support, including through results-based payments, the existing framework as set out in related guidance and decisions already agreed under the Convention for: policy approaches and positive incentives for activities relating to reducing emissions from deforestation and forest degradation, and the role of conservation, sustainable management of forests and enhancement of forest carbon stocks in developing countries; and alternative policy approaches, such as joint mitigation and adaptation approaches for the integral and sustainable management of forests, while reaffirming the importance of incentivizing, as appropriate, non-carbon benefits associated with such approaches.

Article 6

1. Parties recognize that some Parties choose to pursue voluntary cooperation in the implementation of their nationally determined contributions to allow for higher ambition in their mitigation and adaptation actions and to promote sustainable development and environmental integrity.

2. Parties shall, where engaging on a voluntary basis in cooperative approaches that involve the use of internationally transferred mitigation outcomes towards nationally determined contributions, promote sustainable development and ensure

environmental integrity and transparency, including in governance, and shall apply robust accounting to ensure, inter alia, the avoidance of double counting, consistent with guidance adopted by the Conference of the Parties serving as the meeting of the Parties to the Paris Agreement.

3. The use of internationally transferred mitigation outcomes to achieve nationally determined contributions under this Agreement shall be voluntary and authorized by participating Parties.

4. A mechanism to contribute to the mitigation of greenhouse gas emissions and support sustainable development is hereby established under the authority and guidance of the Conference of the Parties serving as the meeting of the Parties to the Paris Agreement for use by Parties on a voluntary basis. It shall be supervised by a body designated by the Conference of the Parties serving as the meeting of the Parties to the Paris Agreement, and shall aim:

(a) To promote the mitigation of greenhouse gas emissions while fostering sustainable development;

(b) To incentivize and facilitate participation in the mitigation of greenhouse gas emissions by public and private entities authorized by a Party;

(c) To contribute to the reduction of emission levels in the host Party, which will benefit from mitigation activities resulting in emission reductions that can also be used by another Party to fulfil its nationally determined contribution; and

(d) To deliver an overall mitigation in global emissions.

5. Emission reductions resulting from the mechanism referred to in paragraph 4 of this Article shall not be used to demonstrate achievement of the host Party's nationally determined

contribution if used by another Party to demonstrate achievement of its nationally determined contribution.

6. The Conference of the Parties serving as the meeting of the Parties to the Paris Agreement shall ensure that a share of the proceeds from activities under the mechanism referred to in paragraph 4 of this Article is used to cover administrative expenses as well as to assist developing country Parties that are particularly vulnerable to the adverse effects of climate change to meet the costs of adaptation.

7. The Conference of the Parties serving as the meeting of the Parties to the Paris Agreement shall adopt rules, modalities and procedures for the mechanism referred to in paragraph 4 of this Article at its first session.

8. Parties recognize the importance of integrated, holistic and balanced non-market approaches being available to Parties to assist in the implementation of their nationally determined contributions, in the context of sustainable development and poverty eradication, in a coordinated and effective manner, including through, inter alia, mitigation, adaptation, finance, technology transfer and capacity-building, as appropriate. These approaches shall aim to:

(a) Promote mitigation and adaptation ambition;

(b) Enhance public and private sector participation in the implementation of nationally determined contributions; and

(c) Enable opportunities for coordination across instruments and relevant institutional arrangements.

9. A framework for non-market approaches to sustainable development is hereby defined to promote the non-market approaches referred to in paragraph 8 of this Article.

Article 7

1. Parties hereby establish the global goal on adaptation of enhancing adaptive capacity, strengthening resilience and reducing vulnerability to climate change, with a view to contributing to sustainable development and ensuring an adequate adaptation response in the context of the temperature goal referred to in Article 2.

2. Parties recognize that adaptation is a global challenge faced by all with local, subnational, national, regional and international dimensions, and that it is a key component of and makes a contribution to the long-term global response to climate change to protect people, livelihoods and ecosystems, taking into account the urgent and immediate needs of those developing country Parties that are particularly vulnerable to the adverse effects of climate change.

3. The adaptation efforts of developing country Parties shall be recognized, in accordance with the modalities to be adopted by the Conference of the Parties serving as the meeting of the Parties to the Paris Agreement at its first session.

4. Parties recognize that the current need for adaptation is significant and that greater levels of mitigation can reduce the need for additional adaptation efforts, and that greater adaptation needs can involve greater adaptation costs.

5. Parties acknowledge that adaptation action should follow a country-driven, gender-responsive, participatory and fully transparent approach, taking into consideration vulnerable groups, communities and ecosystems, and should be based on and guided by the best available science and, as appropriate, traditional knowledge, knowledge of indigenous peoples and local knowledge systems, with a view to integrating adaptation into relevant socioeconomic and environmental policies and actions, where appropriate.

6. Parties recognize the importance of support for and international cooperation on adaptation efforts and the importance of taking into account the needs of developing country Parties, especially those that are particularly vulnerable to the adverse effects of climate change.

7. Parties should strengthen their cooperation on enhancing action on adaptation, taking into account the Cancun Adaptation Framework, including with regard to:

(a) Sharing information, good practices, experiences and lessons learned, including, as appropriate, as these relate to science, planning, policies and implementation in relation to adaptation actions;

(b) Strengthening institutional arrangements, including those under the Convention that serve this Agreement, to support the synthesis of relevant information and knowledge, and the provision of technical support and guidance to Parties;

(c) Strengthening scientific knowledge on climate, including research, systematic observation of the climate system and early warning systems, in a manner that informs climate services and supports decision-making;

(d) Assisting developing country Parties in identifying effective adaptation practices, adaptation needs, priorities, support provided and received for adaptation actions and efforts, and challenges and gaps, in a manner consistent with encouraging good practices;

(e) Improving the effectiveness and durability of adaptation actions.

8. United Nations specialized organizations and agencies are encouraged to support the efforts of Parties to implement the

actions referred to in paragraph 7 of this Article, taking into account the provisions of paragraph 5 of this Article.

9. Each Party shall, as appropriate, engage in adaptation planning processes and the implementation of actions, including the development or enhancement of relevant plans, policies and/or contributions, which may include:

(a) The implementation of adaptation actions, undertakings and/or efforts;

(b) The process to formulate and implement national adaptation plans;

(c) The assessment of climate change impacts and vulnerability, with a view to formulating nationally determined prioritized actions, taking into account vulnerable people, places and ecosystems;

(d) Monitoring and evaluating and learning from adaptation plans, policies, programmes and actions; and

(e) Building the resilience of socioeconomic and ecological systems, including through economic diversification and sustainable management of natural resources.

10. Each Party should, as appropriate, submit and update periodically an adaptation communication, which may include its priorities, implementation and support needs, plans and actions, without creating any additional burden for developing country Parties.

11. The adaptation communication referred to in paragraph 10 of this Article shall be, as appropriate, submitted and updated periodically, as a component of or in conjunction with other communications or documents, including a national adaptation

plan, a nationally determined contribution as referred to in Article 4, paragraph 2, and/or a national communication.

12. The adaptation communications referred to in paragraph 10 of this Article shall be recorded in a public registry maintained by the secretariat.

13. Continuous and enhanced international support shall be provided to developing country Parties for the implementation of paragraphs 7, 9, 10 and 11 of this Article, in accordance with the provisions of Articles 9, 10 and 11.

14. The global stocktake referred to in Article 14 shall, inter alia:

(a) Recognize adaptation efforts of developing country Parties;

(b) Enhance the implementation of adaptation action taking into account the adaptation communication referred to in paragraph 10 of this Article;

(c) Review the adequacy and effectiveness of adaptation and support provided for adaptation; and

(d) Review the overall progress made in achieving the global goal on adaptation referred to in paragraph 1 of this Article.

Article 8

1. Parties recognize the importance of averting, minimizing and addressing loss and damage associated with the adverse effects of climate change, including extreme weather events and slow onset events, and the role of sustainable development in reducing the risk of loss and damage.

2. The Warsaw International Mechanism for Loss and Damage associated with Climate Change Impacts shall be subject to the authority and guidance of the Conference of the Parties serving as the meeting of the Parties to the Paris Agreement and may be

enhanced and strengthened, as determined by the Conference of the Parties serving as the meeting of the Parties to the Paris Agreement.

3. Parties should enhance understanding, action and support, including through the Warsaw International Mechanism, as appropriate, on a cooperative and facilitative basis with respect to loss and damage associated with the adverse effects of climate change.

4. Accordingly, areas of cooperation and facilitation to enhance understanding, action and support may include:

(a) Early warning systems;
(b) Emergency preparedness;
(c) Slow onset events;
(d) Events that may involve irreversible and permanent loss and damage;
(e) Comprehensive risk assessment and management;
(f) Risk insurance facilities, climate risk pooling and other insurance solutions;
(g) Non-economic losses;
(h) Resilience of communities, livelihoods and ecosystems.

5. The Warsaw International Mechanism shall collaborate with existing bodies and expert groups under the Agreement, as well as relevant organizations and expert bodies outside the Agreement.

Article 9

1. Developed country Parties shall provide financial resources to assist developing country Parties with respect to both mitigation and adaptation in continuation of their existing obligations under the Convention.

2. Other Parties are encouraged to provide or continue to provide such support voluntarily.

3. As part of a global effort, developed country Parties should continue to take the lead in mobilizing climate finance from a wide variety of sources, instruments and channels, noting the significant role of public funds, through a variety of actions, including supporting country-driven strategies, and taking into account the needs and priorities of developing country Parties. Such mobilization of climate finance should represent a progression beyond previous efforts.

4. The provision of scaled-up financial resources should aim to achieve a balance between adaptation and mitigation, taking into account country-driven strategies, and the priorities and needs of developing country Parties, especially those that are particularly vulnerable to the adverse effects of climate change and have significant capacity constraints, such as the least developed countries and small island developing States, considering the need for public and grant-based resources for adaptation.

5. Developed country Parties shall biennially communicate indicative quantitative and qualitative information related to paragraphs 1 and 3 of this Article, as applicable, including, as available, projected levels of public financial resources to be provided to developing country Parties. Other Parties providing resources are encouraged to communicate biennially such information on a voluntary basis.

6. The global stocktake referred to in Article 14 shall take into account the relevant information provided by developed country Parties and/or Agreement bodies on efforts related to climate finance.

7. Developed country Parties shall provide transparent and consistent information on support for developing country Parties provided and mobilized through public interventions biennially

in accordance with the modalities, procedures and guidelines to be adopted by the Conference of the Parties serving as the meeting of the Parties to the Paris Agreement, at its first session, as stipulated in Article 13, paragraph 13. Other Parties are encouraged to do so.

8. The Financial Mechanism of the Convention, including its operating entities, shall serve as the financial mechanism of this Agreement.

9. The institutions serving this Agreement, including the operating entities of the Financial Mechanism of the Convention, shall aim to ensure efficient access to financial resources through simplified approval procedures and enhanced readiness support for developing country Parties, in particular for the least developed countries and small island developing States, in the context of their national climate strategies and plans.

Article 10

1. Parties share a long-term vision on the importance of fully realizing technology development and transfer in order to improve resilience to climate change and to reduce greenhouse gas emissions.

2. Parties, noting the importance of technology for the implementation of mitigation and adaptation actions under this Agreement and recognizing existing technology deployment and dissemination efforts, shall strengthen cooperative action on technology development and transfer.

3. The Technology Mechanism established under the Convention shall serve this Agreement.

4. A technology framework is hereby established to provide overarching guidance to the work of the Technology Mechanism

in promoting and facilitating enhanced action on technology development and transfer in order to support the implementation of this Agreement, in pursuit of the long-term vision referred to in paragraph 1 of this Article.

5. Accelerating, encouraging and enabling innovation is critical for an effective, long-term global response to climate change and promoting economic growth and sustainable development. Such effort shall be, as appropriate, supported, including by the Technology Mechanism and, through financial means, by the Financial Mechanism of the Convention, for collaborative approaches to research and development, and facilitating access to technology, in particular for early stages of the technology cycle, to developing country Parties.

6. Support, including financial support, shall be provided to developing country Parties for the implementation of this Article, including for strengthening cooperative action on technology development and transfer at different stages of the technology cycle, with a view to achieving a balance between support for mitigation and adaptation. The global stocktake referred to in Article 14 shall take into account available information on efforts related to support on technology development and transfer for developing country Parties.

Article 11

1. Capacity-building under this Agreement should enhance the capacity and ability of developing country Parties, in particular countries with the least capacity, such as the least developed countries, and those that are particularly vulnerable to the adverse effects of climate change, such as small island developing States, to take effective climate change action, including, inter alia, to implement adaptation and mitigation actions, and should facilitate technology development, dissemination and deployment, access to climate finance, relevant aspects of education, training and public awareness, and

the transparent, timely and accurate communication of information.

2. Capacity-building should be country-driven, based on and responsive to national needs, and foster country ownership of Parties, in particular, for developing country Parties, including at the national, subnational and local levels. Capacity-building should be guided by lessons learned, including those from capacity-building activities under the Convention, and should be an effective, iterative process that is participatory, cross-cutting and gender-responsive.

3. All Parties should cooperate to enhance the capacity of developing country Parties to implement this Agreement. Developed country Parties should enhance support for capacity-building actions in developing country Parties.

4. All Parties enhancing the capacity of developing country Parties to implement this Agreement, including through regional, bilateral and multilateral approaches, shall regularly communicate on these actions or measures on capacity-building. Developing country Parties should regularly communicate progress made on implementing capacity-building plans, policies, actions or measures to implement this Agreement.

5. Capacity-building activities shall be enhanced through appropriate institutional arrangements to support the implementation of this Agreement, including the appropriate institutional arrangements established under the Convention that serve this Agreement. The Conference of the Parties serving as the meeting of the Parties to the Paris Agreement shall, at its first session, consider and adopt a decision on the initial institutional arrangements for capacity-building.

Article 12

Parties shall cooperate in taking measures, as appropriate, to enhance climate change education, training, public awareness, public participation and public access to information, recognizing the importance of these steps with respect to enhancing actions under this Agreement.

Article 13

1. In order to build mutual trust and confidence and to promote effective implementation, an enhanced transparency framework for action and support, with built-in flexibility which takes into account Parties' different capacities and builds upon collective experience is hereby established.

2. The transparency framework shall provide flexibility in the implementation of the provisions of this Article to those developing country Parties that need it in the light of their capacities. The modalities, procedures and guidelines referred to in paragraph 13 of this Article shall reflect such flexibility.

3. The transparency framework shall build on and enhance the transparency arrangements under the Convention, recognizing the special circumstances of the least developed countries and small island developing States, and be implemented in a facilitative, non-intrusive, non-punitive manner, respectful of national sovereignty, and avoid placing undue burden on Parties.

4. The transparency arrangements under the Convention, including national communications, biennial reports and biennial update reports, international assessment and review and international consultation and analysis, shall form part of the experience drawn upon for the development of the modalities, procedures and guidelines under paragraph 13 of this Article.

5. The purpose of the framework for transparency of action is to provide a clear understanding of climate change action in the light of the objective of the Convention as set out in its Article 2,

including clarity and tracking of progress towards achieving Parties' individual nationally determined contributions under Article 4, and Parties' adaptation actions under Article 7, including good practices, priorities, needs and gaps, to inform the global stocktake under Article 14.

6. The purpose of the framework for transparency of support is to provide clarity on support provided and received by relevant individual Parties in the context of climate change actions under Articles 4, 7, 9, 10 and 11, and, to the extent possible, to provide a full overview of aggregate financial support provided, to inform the global stocktake under Article 14.

7. Each Party shall regularly provide the following information:

(a) A national inventory report of anthropogenic emissions by sources and removals by sinks of greenhouse gases, prepared using good practice methodologies accepted by the Intergovernmental Panel on Climate Change and agreed upon by the Conference of the Parties serving as the meeting of the Parties to the Paris Agreement;

(b) Information necessary to track progress made in implementing and achieving its nationally determined contribution under Article 4.

8. Each Party should also provide information related to climate change impacts and adaptation under Article 7, as appropriate.

9. Developed country Parties shall, and other Parties that provide support should, provide information on financial, technology transfer and capacity-building support provided to developing country Parties under Article 9, 10 and 11.

10. Developing country Parties should provide information on financial, technology transfer and capacity-building support needed and received under Articles 9, 10 and 11.

11. Information submitted by each Party under paragraphs 7 and 9 of this Article shall undergo a technical expert review, in accordance with decision 1/CP.21. For those developing country Parties that need it in the light of their capacities, the review process shall include assistance in identifying capacity-building needs. In addition, each Party shall participate in a facilitative, multilateral consideration of progress with respect to efforts under Article 9, and its respective implementation and achievement of its nationally determined contribution.

12. The technical expert review under this paragraph shall consist of a consideration of the Party's support provided, as relevant, and its implementation and achievement of its nationally determined contribution. The review shall also identify areas of improvement for the Party, and include a review of the consistency of the information with the modalities, procedures and guidelines referred to in paragraph 13 of this Article, taking into account the flexibility accorded to the Party under paragraph 2 of this Article. The review shall pay particular attention to the respective national capabilities and circumstances of developing country Parties.

13. The Conference of the Parties serving as the meeting of the Parties to the Paris Agreement shall, at its first session, building on experience from the arrangements related to transparency under the Convention, and elaborating on the provisions in this Article, adopt common modalities, procedures and guidelines, as appropriate, for the transparency of action and support.

14. Support shall be provided to developing countries for the implementation of this Article.

15. Support shall also be provided for the building of transparency-related capacity of developing country Parties on a continuous basis.

Article 14

1. The Conference of the Parties serving as the meeting of the Parties to the Paris Agreement shall periodically take stock of the implementation of this Agreement to assess the collective progress towards achieving the purpose of this Agreement and its long-term goals (referred to as the "global stocktake"). It shall do so in a comprehensive and facilitative manner, considering mitigation, adaptation and the means of implementation and support, and in the light of equity and the best available science.

2. The Conference of the Parties serving as the meeting of the Parties to the Paris Agreement shall undertake its first global stocktake in 2023 and every five years thereafter unless otherwise decided by the Conference of the Parties serving as the meeting of the Parties to the Paris Agreement.

3. The outcome of the global stocktake shall inform Parties in updating and enhancing, in a nationally determined manner, their actions and support in accordance with the relevant provisions of this Agreement, as well as in enhancing international cooperation for climate action.

Article 15

1. A mechanism to facilitate implementation of and promote compliance with the provisions of this Agreement is hereby established.

2. The mechanism referred to in paragraph 1 of this Article shall consist of a committee that shall be expert-based and facilitative in nature and function in a manner that is transparent, non-adversarial and non-punitive. The committee shall pay particular attention to the respective national capabilities and circumstances of Parties.

3. The committee shall operate under the modalities and procedures adopted by the Conference of the Parties serving as the meeting of the Parties to the Paris Agreement at its first

session and report annually to the Conference of the Parties serving as the meeting of the Parties to the Paris Agreement.

Article 16

1. The Conference of the Parties, the supreme body of the Convention, shall serve as the meeting of the Parties to this Agreement.

2. Parties to the Convention that are not Parties to this Agreement may participate as observers in the proceedings of any session of the Conference of the Parties serving as the meeting of the Parties to this Agreement. When the Conference of the Parties serves as the meeting of the Parties to this Agreement, decisions under this Agreement shall be taken only by those that are Parties to this Agreement.

3. When the Conference of the Parties serves as the meeting of the Parties to this Agreement, any member of the Bureau of the Conference of the Parties representing a Party to the Convention but, at that time, not a Party to this Agreement, shall be replaced by an additional member to be elected by and from amongst the Parties to this Agreement.

4. The Conference of the Parties serving as the meeting of the Parties to the Paris Agreement shall keep under regular review the implementation of this Agreement and shall make, within its mandate, the decisions necessary to promote its effective implementation. It shall perform the functions assigned to it by this Agreement and shall:

(a) Establish such subsidiary bodies as deemed necessary for the implementation of this Agreement; and

(b) Exercise such other functions as may be required for the implementation of this Agreement.

5. The rules of procedure of the Conference of the Parties and the financial procedures applied under the Convention shall be applied mutatis mutandis under this Agreement, except as may be otherwise decided by consensus by the Conference of the Parties serving as the meeting of the Parties to the Paris Agreement.

6. The first session of the Conference of the Parties serving as the meeting of the Parties to the Paris Agreement shall be convened by the secretariat in conjunction with the first session of the Conference of the Parties that is scheduled after the date of entry into force of this Agreement. Subsequent ordinary sessions of the Conference of the Parties serving as the meeting of the Parties to the Paris Agreement shall be held in conjunction with ordinary sessions of the Conference of the Parties, unless otherwise decided by the Conference of the Parties serving as the meeting of the Parties to the Paris Agreement.

7. Extraordinary sessions of the Conference of the Parties serving as the meeting of the Parties to the Paris Agreement shall be held at such other times as may be deemed necessary by the Conference of the Parties serving as the meeting of the Parties to the Paris Agreement or at the written request of any Party, provided that, within six months of the request being communicated to the Parties by the secretariat, it is supported by at least one third of the Parties.

8. The United Nations and its specialized agencies and the International Atomic Energy Agency, as well as any State member thereof or observers thereto not party to the Convention, may be represented at sessions of the Conference of the Parties serving as the meeting of the Parties to the Paris Agreement as observers. Any body or agency, whether national or international, governmental or non-governmental, which is qualified in matters covered by this Agreement and which has informed the secretariat of its wish to be represented at a session of the Conference of the Parties serving as the meeting of the

Parties to the Paris Agreement as an observer, may be so admitted unless at least one third of the Parties present object. The admission and participation of observers shall be subject to the rules of procedure referred to in paragraph 5 of this Article.

Article 17

1. The secretariat established by Article 8 of the Convention shall serve as the secretariat of this Agreement.

2. Article 8, paragraph 2, of the Convention on the functions of the secretariat, and Article 8, paragraph 3, of the Convention, on the arrangements made for the functioning of the secretariat, shall apply mutatis mutandis to this Agreement. The secretariat shall, in addition, exercise the functions assigned to it under this Agreement and by the Conference of the Parties serving as the meeting of the Parties to the Paris Agreement.

Article 18

1. The Subsidiary Body for Scientific and Technological Advice and the Subsidiary Body for Implementation established by Articles 9 and 10 of the Convention shall serve, respectively, as the Subsidiary Body for Scientific and Technological Advice and the Subsidiary Body for Implementation of this Agreement. The provisions of the Convention relating to the functioning of these two bodies shall apply mutatis mutandis to this Agreement. Sessions of the meetings of the Subsidiary Body for Scientific and Technological Advice and the Subsidiary Body for Implementation of this Agreement shall be held in conjunction with the meetings of, respectively, the Subsidiary Body for Scientific and Technological Advice and the Subsidiary Body for Implementation of the Convention.

2. Parties to the Convention that are not Parties to this Agreement may participate as observers in the proceedings of any session of the subsidiary bodies. When the subsidiary bodies

serve as the subsidiary bodies of this Agreement, decisions under this Agreement shall be taken only by those that are Parties to this Agreement.

3. When the subsidiary bodies established by Articles 9 and 10 of the Convention exercise their functions with regard to matters concerning this Agreement, any member of the bureaux of those subsidiary bodies representing a Party to the Convention but, at that time, not a Party to this Agreement, shall be replaced by an additional member to be elected by and from amongst the Parties to this Agreement.

Article 19

1. Subsidiary bodies or other institutional arrangements established by or under the Convention, other than those referred to in this Agreement, shall serve this Agreement upon a decision of the Conference of the Parties serving as the meeting of the Parties to the Paris Agreement. The Conference of the Parties serving as the meeting of the Parties to the Paris Agreement shall specify the functions to be exercised by such subsidiary bodies or arrangements.

2. The Conference of the Parties serving as the meeting of the Parties to the Paris Agreement may provide further guidance to such subsidiary bodies and institutional arrangements.

Article 20

1. This Agreement shall be open for signature and subject to ratification, acceptance or approval by States and regional economic integration organizations that are Parties to the Convention. It shall be open for signature at the United Nations Headquarters in New York from 22 April 2016 to 21 April 2017. Thereafter, this Agreement shall be open for accession from the day following the date on which it is closed for signature.

Instruments of ratification, acceptance, approval or accession shall be deposited with the Depositary.

2. Any regional economic integration organization that becomes a Party to this Agreement without any of its member States being a Party shall be bound by all the obligations under this Agreement. In the case of regional economic integration organizations with one or more member States that are Parties to this Agreement, the organization and its member States shall decide on their respective responsibilities for the performance of their obligations under this Agreement. In such cases, the organization and the member States shall not be entitled to exercise rights under this Agreement concurrently.

3. In their instruments of ratification, acceptance, approval or accession, regional economic integration organizations shall declare the extent of their competence with respect to the matters governed by this Agreement. These organizations shall also inform the Depositary, who shall in turn inform the Parties, of any substantial modification in the extent of their competence.

Article 21

1. This Agreement shall enter into force on the thirtieth day after the date on which at least 55 Parties to the Convention accounting in total for at least an estimated 55 percent of the total global greenhouse gas emissions have deposited their instruments of ratification, acceptance, approval or accession.

2. Solely for the limited purpose of paragraph 1 of this Article, "total global greenhouse gas emissions" means the most up-to-date amount communicated on or before the date of adoption of this Agreement by the Parties to the Convention.

3. For each State or regional economic integration organization that ratifies, accepts or approves this Agreement or accedes

thereto after the conditions set out in paragraph 1 of this Article for entry into force have been fulfilled, this Agreement shall enter into force on the thirtieth day after the date of deposit by such State or regional economic integration organization of its instrument of ratification, acceptance, approval or accession.

4. For the purposes of paragraph 1 of this Article, any instrument deposited by a regional economic integration organization shall not be counted as additional to those deposited by its member States.

Article 22

The provisions of Article 15 of the Convention on the adoption of amendments to the Convention shall apply mutatis mutandis to this Agreement.

Article 23

1. The provisions of Article 16 of the Convention on the adoption and amendment of annexes to the Convention shall apply mutatis mutandis to this Agreement.

2. Annexes to this Agreement shall form an integral part thereof and, unless otherwise expressly provided for, a reference to this Agreement constitutes at the same time a reference to any annexes thereto. Such annexes shall be restricted to lists, forms and any other material of a descriptive nature that is of a scientific, technical, procedural or administrative character.

Article 24

The provisions of Article 14 of the Convention on settlement of disputes shall apply mutatis mutandis to this Agreement.

Article 25

1. Each Party shall have one vote, except as provided for paragraph 2 of this Article.

2. Regional economic integration organizations, in matters within their competence, shall exercise their right to vote with a number of votes equal to the number of their member States that are Parties to this Agreement. Such an organization shall not exercise its right to vote if any of its member States exercises its right, and vice versa.

Article 26

The Secretary-General of the United Nations shall be the Depositary of this Agreement.

Article 27

No reservations may be made to this Agreement.

Article 28

1. At any time after three years from the date on which this Agreement has entered into force for a Party, that Party may withdraw from this Agreement by giving written notification to the Depositary.

2. Any such withdrawal shall take effect upon expiry of one year from the date of receipt by the Depositary of the notification of withdrawal, or on such later date as may be specified in the notification of withdrawal.

3. Any Party that withdraws from the Convention shall be considered as also having withdrawn from this Agreement.

Article 29

The original of this Agreement, of which the Arabic, Chinese, English, French, Russian and Spanish texts are equally authentic, shall be deposited with the Secretary-General of the United Nations.

DONE at Paris this twelfth day of December two thousand and fifteen.

IN WITNESS WHEREOF, the undersigned, being duly authorized to that effect, have signed this Agreement.

About the Author

Albert K. Bates is a retired public interest attorney and author of several books on energy, environment, and history. He is a co-founder of the Ecovillage Network of the Americas and the Global Ecovillage Network. During his 26-year career as an attorney, he argued environmental and civil rights cases before the US Supreme Court and drafted a number of legislative acts while publishing *Natural Rights,* a quarterly newsletter on deep ecology. His books *Shutdown: Nuclear Power on Trial* (1979) and *Climate in Crisis: The Greenhouse Effect and What You Can Do* (1990, with foreword by Al Gore) provided early insight into two of the greatest dangers now confronting the world. In 1980 he shared the first Right Livelihood Award for his work with Plenty International in preserving indigenous cultures. An inveterate inventor, he holds a number of design patents and was designer of concentrating photovoltaic arrays and solar-hybrid automobiles displayed at the 1982 World's Fair. He has been director of the Global Village Institute for Appropriate Technology since 1984 and of the Ecovillage Training Center at The Farm community in Summertown, Tennessee, since 1994, where he has taught natural building, sustainable agriculture, permaculture and appropriate technology to students from more than 50 nations. His books, *The Post-Petroleum Survival Guide and Cookbook* (with foreword by Richard Heinberg) and *The Biochar Solution: Carbon Farming and Climate Change* (with foreword by Vandana Shiva) are available in print and all e-book formats from New Society Publishers. A series of books, the ecovillage imprint, collecting his investigatory research and reporting over 30 years is available on Amazon for Kindle. Most recent additions are *Pour Evian on Your Radishes* and *The Paris Agreement.* He blogs at *The Great Change* and tweets *@peaksurfer.* A YouTube channel is available at the Collapse Café.

Portrait by Jack Wein

www.ingramcontent.com/pod-product-compliance
Lightning Source LLC
Chambersburg PA
CBHW060253100426
42742CB00011B/1740